D0534922

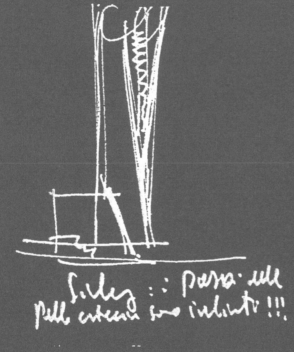

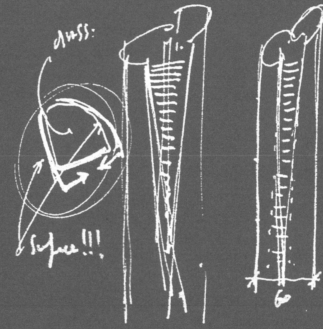

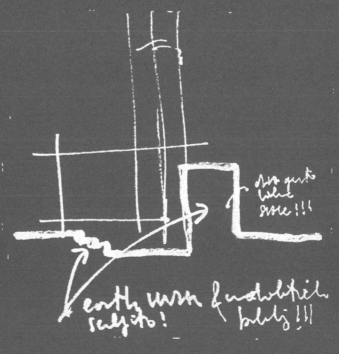

Aurora Place Renzo Piano Sydney

Aurora Place Renzo Piano Sydney

Andrew Metcalf

Photographs by
Martin van der Wal

The Watermark Press

A Watermark Press Book

First published in Australia
and New Zealand in 2001 by
The Watermark Press Pty Limited,
Sydney, Australia

Copyright © Text: Andrew Metcalf
© Photographs: Martin van der Wal

This book is copyright. Apart from any fair
dealing for the purposes of private study,
research, criticism or review as permitted
under the Copyright Act 1968, no part may
be stored or reproduced by any process
without prior written permission. Enquiries
should be made to the publisher.

National Library of Australia Cataloguing-in-
Publication Data

Metcalf, Andrew.
Aurora Place, Sydney.

Includes index.
ISBN 0 949284 53 X
1. Tall buildings – Design and construction.
2. Architecture – Designs and plans.
I. Wal, Martin van der.
II. Title

721.042

Editor: Simon Blackall
Associate Editor: Carl Schibrowski
Design: Carl Martin with Danielle Powell
and Michelina Evangelista

Colour separation in Hong Kong by International Lithographic
Manufactured in China by Imago

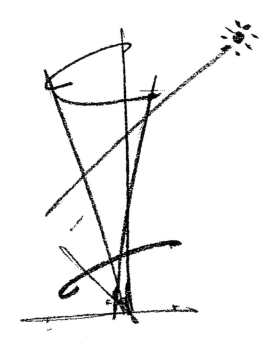

Contents

16   **Introduction**

20   **Context**

30   **Process**
       36   Logistical Web

38   **Architectural Analysis**
       50   Structural Framing
       58   Geometry
       62   Ground Plane
       66   Wintergardens
       70   Residential Building

80   **Technology**
       88   Lifts/Elevators

90   **Light**
       96   Commercial Tower Facades
       98   Glass

102   **Product**
       106   Commercial Lobby
       112   Terracotta
       114   Canopy
       118   Piazza

122   **Place**
       128   Exterior Lighting
       130   BMU

132   **Expression**

136   **Art**

146   **Acknowledgements**

148   **Index**

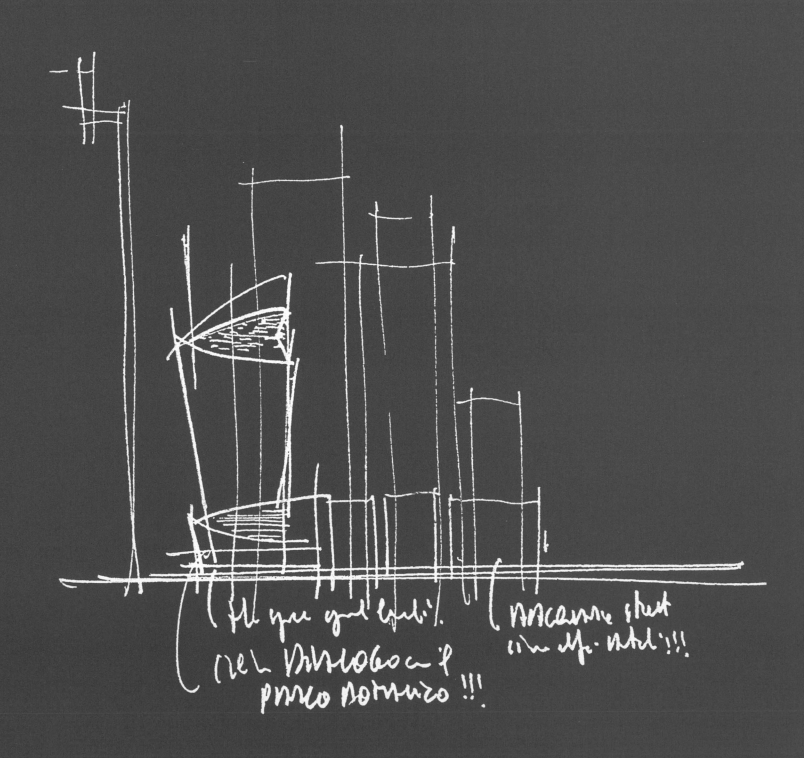

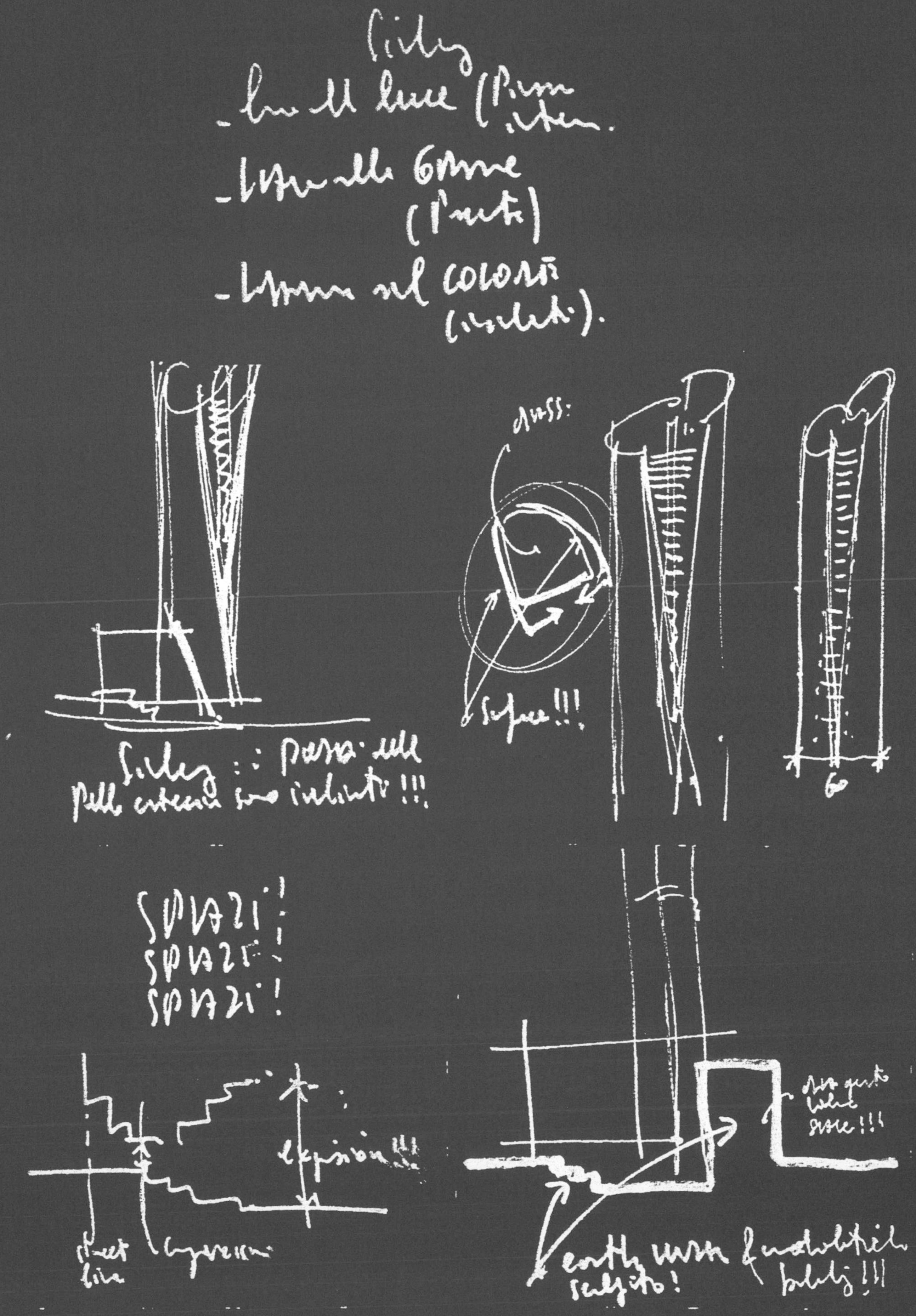
SPAZI!
SPAZI!
SPAZI!
60
street line

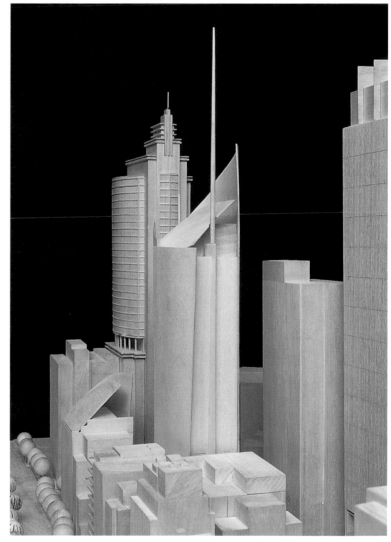

EAST ELEVATION

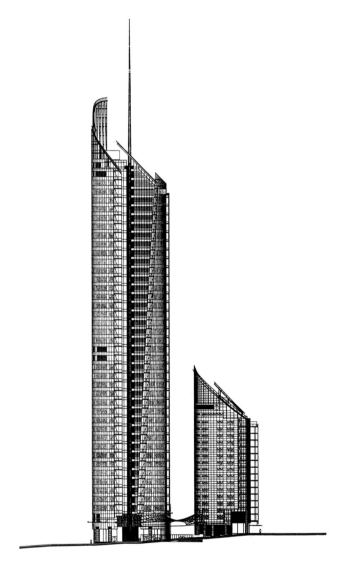

SOUTH ELEVATION

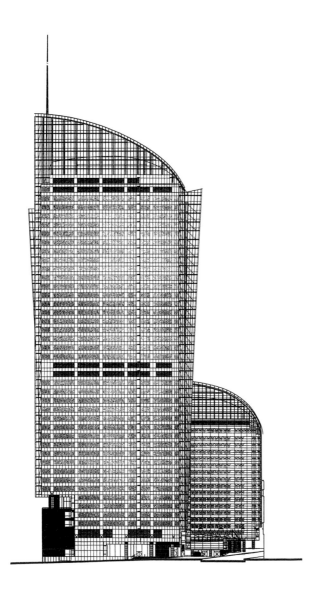

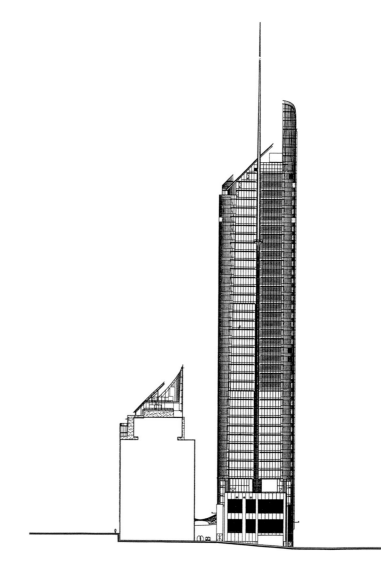

WEST ELEVATION

NORTH ELEVATION

Introduction

In the taxonomy of cities there are harbour cities and river cities. Sydney is a harbour city, not a river city and a quick look at its harbour makes the difference clear. Sydney's other distinguishing trait is that, compared to other places, it has a superfluity of sunshine and a keenness of light. The city's particular beauty rests with its memorable harbour and its sharp light. Both are like no other. The harbour appears as a huge island of sea water dramatically wedged into a hilly, rocky coastline. It reaches up to and metamorphoses into a myriad of creeks and gullies where fresh water meets salt and suburban houses meet thick bushland. Along the way the city has built up web upon web of suburbs connected by roads that originally followed the ridges for fear of the steep land. Of course the sun doesn't shine all the time—in fact the nation's oldest city has a high rainfall—but stormy weather doesn't persist, and a strong, unfiltered sunlight has jurisdiction for most of the year.

The harbour is amazing to look at from any angle or height and its scale is wondrous: no single work of architecture or engineering apart from the Opera House and the Harbour Bridge, seems to have made an impact. More recently these two have been joined by another impressive, feat of construction, the harbour tunnel. Here, it is not a privileged sense of vision, but one's sense of elapsed travelling time, which conveys great size and scale.

If most individual works are aesthetically silent, around the perimeter of this vast harbour, the spreading accretions of the suburbs offer the only substantial balance to the world of water, light and fauna. Here, the challenge for architecture is as obvious as it is daunting. Build in this place and understand that it is not just the historical city, but scale, light and nature itself that are at issue. It is a place to commemorate Corbusier's dictum that '…our eyes are constructed to enable us to see forms in light.'[1]

Sydney's recent history of commercial architecture has yielded a lot of commerce and just a few works of architecture, the works of Harry Seidler and Denton Corker Marshall among them. At its centre the clutch of tall office buildings stands in a powerful dialectical relationship to the harbour, but at the cost of a virtual exclusion of nature itself. Light is shared by closely packed, buildings that, ironically, jostle one another to share a precious commodity - a view of the harbour.

Not more than 20 years ago in Sydney, the conventional wisdom was that the best parts of the central business district for a Grade A, commercial office development were somewhere within walking distance of the Stock Exchange, or close to Circular Quay and the harbour. In fact, the harbour, or views of it, was really the defining desirable characteristic. Endowed with such a site and with harbour views, it was said, a good building could attract top rent for its upper floors and return a healthy profit on development costs.

On the other hand, at that time Macquarie Street, one of the city's oldest streets with a noticeable complement of smaller, heritage buildings and a sole remaining apartment building [the Astor Flats, built in the 1920s], was predominantly a place of government and public capital.

The Aurora Place site, at the junction of Macquarie and Bent streets, was formerly occupied by the State Government Office Block. Today, just further south, institutions like the State Parliament and Library, Sydney Hospital and the Reserve Bank still grace Macquarie Street. Twenty years ago this street, named for the most enlightened of colonial governors, was too far away from the bourse and too heavily protected by heritage orders for its real estate to be of interest to serious developers.

Now, quite suddenly, the State Office Block is no longer, the Astor Flats have been joined by a new 11 storey apartment building on Macquarie Street and a new office building which reaches a height of 44 floors behind it. Other new apartment buildings and smaller office towers face Macquarie Street at various points along its length.

So what has changed? What has changed is not the replacement but the co-habitation of private with public capital in this part of the city. The development by Lend Lease and the East Asia Property Group of Aurora Place designed by the Genoa-based architect Renzo Piano Building Workshop (RPBW), is perhaps the most spectacular example of this change and the topic of this book. It was the developers' recognition of Piano's body of work spanning 30 years, and the fact that each project was unique and appropriate to its context that decided the commission. In a number of ways the project can be characterised as a frontier type, in the sense that 'frontier' can mean initial, first, at the sharp edge of developments and ideas etc. The frontier elements here begin with the site itself. It is on an edge of Sydney's central business district in a place which, hitherto, had been the tightly held preserve of the New South Wales State Government, but now, in the way of

public/private business heterogeneity and the transfer of public assets, is perceptibly a private place. Then there is the mix of residential and office components, which is unusual for Sydney. Add to that an architect, who is internationally renowned, undertaking his first commission in Australia and his first building over 20 floors in height [the commercial tower is 44 floors plus the 'crown']. Also, the architecture represents a frontier of the 'contextual' approach for Piano: its literal reference to the roof forms of Utzon's famous Opera House nearby make this design perhaps the most mimetically ornamental of Piano's works. Then there are the new ideas about office life that have led to the provision of 'break-out' spaces, or perhaps more aptly described as high rise conservatories. Finally there is the deployment of materials such as glass and terracotta, which position Aurora Place at the frontier of constructional technology.

The plan of this book has a main text in chapter format interspersed with more detailed information shown in italics. It begins with an examination of historical, topographical physical context, the Macquarie Street location in Sydney with some reference to the particular site at the corner of Bent and Macquarie Streets. The next chapter deals with the RPBW way of working in collaboration with the client/developer. For these architects the operating process—nicely alluded to in the use of the term 'workshop'—is significant. Piano himself refers to it as an 'open university'. Indeed, it is a place where 600 different young architects have worked together over the past few decades. In a most successful collaboration with Lend Lease Design Group, the project manager, the engineering consultants and the construction company, they produced a

significant world-class building withisn time and on budget. The third chapter gives an architectural analysis of Aurora Place in the light of such things as precedents [within and without Piano's work] and the architectural achievements that emerge. The next two chapters, 'Technology' followed by 'Light' include a discussion of two aspects that are commonly raised, both by Piano and by other commentators in the discourse on his architecture. However here the task is to try and position the discussion more generally within the history of ideas including the large literature on technology [particularly in philosophy], and in the case of Light, I've attempted to locate the discussion within ideas coming from the Enlightenment. In a short interlude, the next chapter, 'Product', examines the industrial design aspect of Piano's work. Then the concluding chapters 'Place' followed by 'Expression' return to the interpretive framework developed within the history of ideas, not architecture. However, architecture is about 'place-making' and this interpretive device is surely valid in a section on place. Architecture is also about 'expression' and, although Renzo Piano is cautious about expession, it may be argued that Aurora Place may be amongst the most expressive or sculptural of his works.

Aurora Place is situated on an architectural and technological frontier. In these terms it succeeds in a way that no other recent project in the city does. Along the way it raises issues about technology, light and context and architectural expression that only a work by Piano could. It also fulfilled Lend Lease's highest aspirations for the site—an early landmark for the new millennium.

1 Le Corbusier, [1927]
Towards a New Architecture

Context

OPPOSITE The gradually expanding floor width of the commercial tower at Aurora Place is clearly noticeable in the left of the picture.

'...every kind of building has a different story and is in a different place...'[1]

The story of Aurora Place, begins with the city itself and Macquarie Street, a large boulevard that connects two significant city features, Hyde Park and the harbour; the one pure artifice and the other a natural wonder. The park positioned between the edge of the central business district and its immediate periphery, and the harbour forming an edge to the city's northward extension. From colonial history we know that this broad avenue is named for Governor Lachlan Macquarie [1761–1824] a Scottish colonel with a taste for the literature of Scott and Boswell. Macquarie was a scion of the English enlightenment, who believed in the regeneration of convicts through their deployment on public works. He was Governor-in-Chief of New South Wales and van Dieman's land, during a period of strong growth, from 1810 to 1821 and his most topical and divisive administrative outcome was to introduce a system of emancipation, freeing convicts after the expiration or remission of their sentences. Macquarie, who placed order higher than democracy, despaired at the ramshackle layout of Sydney's buildings and streets and set about instituting a system of wide, straight streets, the eastern most of which is the one that bears his name.

At the time of the governor's departure Macquarie Street terminated at its junction with Bent Street[2], today, the site of Aurora Place. Having arrived at this point a traveller in the early 1820s stood before the grounds of the 'Governor's Domain' as it was known, of Government House which covered all the land north to the harbour and from today's Circular Quay to Woolloomooloo Bay including Sydney Cove and Farm Cove. On one peninsular in this vast landscaped space stood Fort Macquarie, which was eventually demolished to construct the Sydney Opera House at Bennelong Point. At the tip of the other, and still unchanged, is the site of Mrs Macquarie's Chair, then a private belvedere and place of solitude for the first lady of the colony.

ABOVE Looking north along Macquarie Street to the new apartment building. OPPOSITE MAIN IMAGE Looking upwards at the Macquarie Apartments from the south-east with the wintergardens and the glass louvres clearly visible.

In an 1823 map, the Aurora Place site was vacant government land and the site of today's State Library was designated as 'Greenway's site for Government House'. In any event, during his tenure, Macquarie codified the land-use pattern of public and government buildings along the whole of the eastern side of Macquarie Street. One must carefully keep in mind, that, at that time, this was the whole of Macquarie Street, i.e. from Hyde Park to Bent Street. This government 'zone' is thus one of the longest standing extant land usages in the city of Sydney.

The extension of Macquarie Street further north was close at hand. By 1838, when a crew-member of the French ship *La Venus* drew the town's plan[3], he showed the proposed transfer of the whole south-west corner section of the Governor's Domain to the growing city. This included the extension of Macquarie and Phillip Streets northward to Farm Cove, together with Loftus and Young Streets two new parallel pieces of a new regular grid that would stretch between George and Macquarie Streets. By this time plans were afoot to construct a new Government House which was to be the present one supervised by the architect Mortimer Lewis in the mid 1840s. At the corner of Macquarie and Bent Streets, de Thierry's map showed a new public building, The Australian Subscription Library, on the site now occupied by the new Macquarie Apartments with a vacant site adjoining it in Phillip Street. Opposite it at about the entry point to today's Royal Botanical Gardens [the southern end of the Governor's Domain] the French map showed the *Bureaux Publics* a long, building with its thin end facing west.

Thus, the Aurora Place site once occupied a place on the boundary or frontier of the nascent city, as it was then. Although 'frontier' normally implies the edge beyond which uncharted land beckons, it is meant in this case to suggest a demarcation line between public and private land, and between built and landscape spaces in the urban framework. Fortunately the developers, Lend Lease, recognised and understood the history and importance of the site and chose an architect who, it was hoped, would be able to create the type of building that would find a place in the history of the built environment.

After another 50 years the story had changed again—it was 1888, the year of Australia's centenary of European settlement. In the intervening years the colonial administration had added to its stock of prestige public buildings on Macquarie Street with the [former] Treasury [1849, now the Intercontinental Hotel] on the corner of Bridge Street and, opposite it, the Chief Secretary's Department [1878], conveniently close to Government House. Along the western side of Macquarie Street between Bent and Bridge Streets, a fine row of neo-Georgian and Victorian townhouses appeared; most of them have gone now but two that remain are No 145, the Royal Australian College of Physicians [before 1848] and History House at No 133 [1853]. Six years before the centennial the burgeoning new city lost the Garden Palace, an ambitious reworking of London's Crystal Palace, to fire. Sited in the southern section of the Botanical gardens across from the Aurora Place site, the Garden Palace hosted an international industrial exhibition and included Sydney's first hydraulic lift in its north tower.[5] A panoramic photograph taken from its roof shows a glimpse of the Aurora Place site with a 4/6 storey masonry building wrapped around the corner.

NEAR RIGHT View from the top of the apartment building looking through the 450 roff louvre system to the Mitchell Library and the Domain parklands beyond. RIGHT The eastern facade of the commercial tower building seen from across the water at Farm Cove.
OPPOSITE PAGE Looking east from Aurora Place across the Royal Botanic Gardens with Farm Cove just visible at the top left of the picture.

FOLLOWING PAGE View from the top of the commercial tower, looking past the north-east fin, which is supported by a cantilevered leaf spring (right foreground) which holds the panellised curtain wall system in place.

In a magnificent 1888 aerial lithograph print of the 'City of Sydney' by M.S.Hill can be seen what looks to be this building with the NSW Government Printer's building behind. This is the site of the Aurora Place office tower today.[6]

Thus, ownership of the site always seems to have been in public hands, as it still is. After the Government Printer and the Australian Subscription Library came the State Office Block. It was built to the designs of the Government Architect in 1967 and, until it was demolished to make way for the Aurora Place development, was home to the NSW Premier, some ministers and the once-large Public Works Department of New South Wales.

In 1888 Macquarie Street was decked out with wood and plaster triumphal arches for the colony's centennial celebrations that included the unveiling of a statue of Queen Victoria which stands today just off Macquarie Street in St James' Square.

Then, after another 30 years, Sydney received a visit from the English novelist, D.H. Lawrence:

'A bunch of workmen were lying on the grass of the park in Macquarie Street, in the dinner hour. It was winter, the end of May, but the sun was warm, and they lay there in shirts sleeves, talking. Some were eating food from paper packages. They were a mixed lot—taxi drivers, a group of builders who were putting a new inside into one of the big houses opposite, and then two men in blue overalls, some sort of mechanics. Squatting and lying on the grassy bank beside the broad tarred road where taxis and hansom cabs passed continually, they had that air of owning the city which belongs to a good Australian. Sometimes, from the distance behind them, came the faintest singing from out of the 'fortified' Conservatorium of Music.'[7] *(continued on page 28)*

Today, in Macquarie Street, the same grassy bank offers a lunch spot for a more diverse groups of workers and the same Conservatorium nurtures young musical talent.

Although, nothing of the music, not even a squeak, can be heard above the sound of traffic and the city's perceptible hum. As you walk or drive up Bent Street towards Macquarie Street, the buildings on either side hem in one's gaze, and then when you reach Macquarie Street the proscenium opens up with a clear view across the valley to Potts Point. From here with the gardens and the State Library on either side, the experience is one of approaching an edge. The site seems like no other. Remarkably, it still has the feel of a gateway that it must have held 150 years ago before Macquarie Street was pushed through the Domain to Sydney Cove.

Architecture is local by definition, local in the etymological sense, i.e. limited to the place, the topography, the terrain. [Renzo Piano]

For Piano the topography of Aurora Place emerges from the site's relationship to the harbour and to the Opera House on Bennelong Point. At the start of design in 1996 he quickly took hold of the relationship and it became a point of departure. In a cryptic simplification of the topography, the architect's idiomatic sketch depicting the relationship shows both the tower building and the Opera House on the same level, indicating that Jorn Utzon's famous design was something of an aesthetic benchmark. Piano alludes to this in one of the many interviews he recorded at the time he received the Pritzker Prize in 1998:

I believe the tower in Sydney…will be my most high-tech design. It has to be when you have the Opera House as the city's trademark.[9]

If the north-south slice is one way to look at the site's topography, the east-west section through Sydney is just as interesting. Macquarie Street is one of the ridge lines which give the city its form; York Street, Macquarie Street, Art Gallery Road and Victoria Street are the four parallel ridges all running towards the harbour which, in a way, prescribe the map of downtown Sydney. Typical of the sandstone geographic structure of the Sydney region, they are spaced at relatively regular intervals, originally with water courses between them, draining into the coves of the harbour. To the early colonial administrators these ridges became the set out points for the street system—the deep structure of the city. Subsequent development of built form, especially with high rise towers, has reinforced this undulating topography. York Street is a powerful urban form because of its alignment with the bridge and its tight enclosure of buildings; similarly, Macquarie Street has a strong presence through its broad, open spatial character, incorporating many public buildings and its termination at the Opera House forecourt. Art Gallery Road is perhaps the antinomy, but has a quiet presence on its own, and Victoria Street, the tallest and the most dramatic, walls in the city's eastern horizon.

Aurora Place, viewed from these ridges, with its sail-like facades and scalloped crowns, is an arresting, welcome new addition to the city form. In his *Logbook* Piano attested that '…the tower will be a homage to the city'[10], and though he has paid homage through the city's 'trademark', Aurora Place's form, produced by Piano and made possible by the Lend lease Design Group and constructed by Bovis Lend Lease, brings to mind the work of the Danish master.

Piano has also said that '... new projects in a young city like Sydney should really seek a very powerful role; they should complete and solidify an urban fabric that is not yet completely settled.'[11] The company of neighbouring buildings that Aurora Place solidifies is not undistinguished. Most notable is the slightly larger Chifley Tower directly across Bent Street, designed by Kohn Pederson Fox in the late 1980s. And, across Phillip Street, the architecturally distinguished Governor Macquarie Tower, Governor Phillip tower and the Museum of Sydney built on the site of the First Government House and completed in 1994 by architects Denton Corker Marshall.

From the vantage point of the ridges, particularly those to the east, or from the harbour itself, the young city these towers make is indeed solid. It is also scenographic as it steps back with a verdant foreground of the Domain and then the low-rise development along Macquarie Street topped off by the skyscrapers behind. Thus the Aurora Place site has three topographical components: the Opera House axis, the four ridge lines and these stepping terraces. These terraces, incidentally, figure in the micro climatic environment as well. In the Sydney climate eastern orientation ensures two complementary phenomena: sunshine and sea-breezes. At Aurora Place these too have become design ingredients, firstly in the development of the apartment wintergardens facing the street and, secondly, in the office tower wintergardens which act as social spaces on each level. RPBW's laudable intention in both instances was to allow inhabitants to have unrestricted access to the sun and the breeze without the dulling presence of hermetic sealing and air-conditioning that is the orthodoxy of other buildings.

Taken as a 200 year history, the physical and conceptual frontiers of this site and the buildings on it haven't been frozen in one state for long at all, but have melted and re-emerged in different forms over time. The State Office Block, built with long-lasting bronze cladding, survived for a mere thirty years. Today the dissolution and re-emerging have produced a multi-function commercial development that, through its financial backing and its architecture is trans-national in character and should be seen in a world context. The speed of change is fast, almost equal to that of the global flow of capital and services that created it. Now it is normal for our identities—national, cultural, regional and individual to experience the tension of dissolution and re-assembly that the Aurora Place story tells.

1 Interview of Renzo Piano in the 'Jim Lehrer News Hour,' 19th June, 1998.
2 Plan of the Town and Suburbs of Sydney, August 1822. Photocopy in author's collection. Also Plan of Sydney, 1823 published in A.W. Jose, *Builders and Pioneers of Australia*.
3 Sydney in 1838, Map published in Abel du Petit-Thouar [1841] *Voyage autour du monde sur la fregate La Venus, pendant les annees 1836–1839*.
4 Interview of Renzo Piano in the 'Jim Lehrer News Hour,' 19th June, 1998.
5 *Sydney Vistas, Panoramic Views 1788–1995*, Museum of Sydney, 1995.
6 Ibid, p29.
7 D. H. Lawrence [1923] *Kangaroo* p1.
8 Renzo Piano [1997] *Logbook* p249.
9 Bonnie Churchill, 'Diverse Projects Cover Italian's Drawing Board', *Christian Science Monitor*, 24th April, 1998.
10 *Logbook*, p242.
11 Ibid

Process

OPPOSITE Scale models made of materials that will represent the final concept are an important part of the design process.

I insist on the need to engage in a multi-disciplinarity based on handcraft.

When I speak of the need to listen I don't mean just to the clients or colleagues, but also to the engineer and the scientist working with you. In talking about a new craftmanship and about reacquiring the design process in its integrity, I view this capacity to combine different experiences in the creative process, not in a theoretical sense but in a serious manner, also as a stage which must be gone through for one to achieve serious architecture.[1]

The architecture of the RPBW is not a style that can be instantly recognised, but an architecture that emerges through a specific team-based process. Piano has established rules of architectural practice which, certainly on Aurora Place, helped to build the dynamic relationship with the developer/clients. By drawing on the contributions of many and synthesising them to a point that the resultant work has an authenticity and rationale that might only otherwise emerge from the mind of one, the RPBW has consistently succeeded in forging cohesive partnerships. The real challenge of large architectural projects is to somehow progress them and still maintain design integrity at the general and detail scales of operation. The example of an accomplished architect working solo on a high quality small project is appropriate. How do you approach that particular level of integration and rationale in a building with hundreds of people working on it?

The RPBW process, which has been described in detail elsewhere,[2] began with Piano's experiences at the Pompidou Centre in Paris in the early 1970s, working jointly with Richard Rogers in an inter-disciplinary relationship with the structural engineer, Peter Rice and the building contractors. Shortly thereafter Piano's work embraced the activity of architectural research where he pursued a deep interest in construction as a quasi-theoretical activity. Here again collaborative, work with inputs from specialists and a rigorous scientific-based method were crucial in vindicating the experimental nature of the projects.[4]

OPPOSITE These typical CAD models play an important part in defining the shape of the, as yet, unbuilt commercial tower at Aurora Place.

32 Process

In his early high profile projects like the Menil Museum in Houston [1982–86] and the IBM Travelling Pavilion [1982–84] Piano responded to the challenge of meeting complex architectural briefs, with innovative designs and sophisticated constructional technology in widely separate geographic sites. Piano did this by developing a method for correlating specific themes and dealing with them in consistent ways that nonetheless respond to the specificity of each project. Piano says right from the start on a project he '…thinks about materials, modes and *tekne*…'[4], but he also says that it is not usual for him to start designing straight away:

I feel bound by a kind of discipline to restrain myself and allow elements to accumulate for a while, sometimes over quite a long period. When the projects are of a highly complex nature they need to be assimilated slowly; knowledge needs to be stored up and you need to wait in silence…[5]

Themes such as site context, climate, history, street connectivity, 'lightness', structural framing, cladding and panelling, glazing, roofs-as-light and so on are typical of the Piano elements or themes. The writer Kenneth Frampton considers this capacity to break a building project down into its constituent parts to be a 'mastery over the means of production' which underpins '…an appropriate character of the work in hand'.[6]

The Building Workshop process then is definitely not that of a solitary architect, but one that requires time and the combined skills of various people, including consultants and relevant others. Piano has talked of the Workshop as an open university '…deliberately composed of 45–50 persons, the widest range which allows a creative relationship with each individual.' However he doesn't '…believe in the effectiveness of participation understood as so many people around a table, each voicing his own opinion'. He feels, in the end, the architect can't abrogate the specific responsibility of providing form.[7] In fact the process is a synergistic and iterative one which requires of its participants an ability to listen as well as talk. At the end of such a process it is not possible to say with certainty who did what. Piano, who makes sketches, but doesn't work on the drawing board or computer, refers to the synthesis stage as a stitching together which is preceded by a period of consultation, silence, dialogue and research, resulting in sketches and work notes[8].

After the 'stitching together' Piano watches and guides others working up the design. He favours clear, so-called 'technical' drawings over the more seductive, rhetorical architectural renderings [which often contain a distracting subjectivity]. Technical drawings can be dispassionately assessed, and probably, like scientific illustrations, are more likely to reflect the collaborative context in which the designs are created. The production of technical drawings also ensures construction and detailing issues are addressed. It also allows a quicker phasing in of precise models and mock-ups which are another fundamental part of the Piano process. Ideas are tested not just in the two dimensional confines of a drawing but in mathematical calculations and accurately in models of all scales before they are deemed 'tested' much in the way that prototypes are in industrial design.

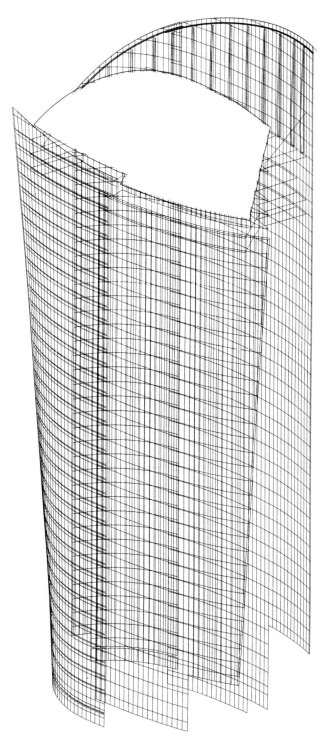

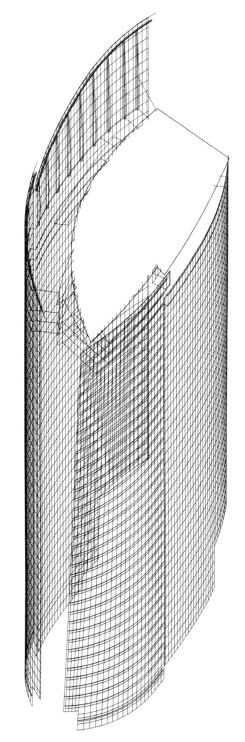

3D Image - view from North East

3D Image - view from South East

33

While self-conscious collaboration, consultation and precision are obvious key words in any description of the Piano process, what stands out is the ethic of craftmanship and the intent to reacquire the design process, as he puts it. The suggestion here that many architects have lost their way and not discharged key responsibilities warrants close attention:

Unless an architect is able to listen to people and understand them he may simply be someone who creates architecture for his own fame and self-glorification instead of doing the real work he has to do ... An architect must be a craftsman...These days the tools might include a computer, an experimental model and mathematics. However, it is still craftsman ship—the work of someone who does not separate the work of the mind from the work of the hand. It involves a circular process that draws you from an idea to a drawing, from a drawing to an experiment, from experiment to construction and from construction back to an idea again. For me this cycle is fundamental to creative work. Unfortunately many have come to accept these steps as independent... Teamwork is essential if creative projects are to come about. Teamwork requires an ability to listen and engage in a dialogue.[11]

The cyclical or iterative aspect is obviously crucial. Part of the reacquiring of the design activity is to build a method that is iterative and verifies quality at certain points in the process. Cycling can also include reference to precedents. Over time the Workshop has developed a series of tectonic tropes that have now become recognisable and highly evolved architecturally to become 'products' characterised by the Workshop's design precision and craft. Their use on projects is not random but fundamental to discharging

an architectural responsibility. Examples of these products that enrich the experience of the Sydney design include the terracotta cladding and louvres, the thermal cushion glass walls to the apartment building and the suspended glass roof to the piazza. Before commissioning RPBW the developers, who had vast experience in the construction of high-rise commercial buildings, considered several other internationally-recognised architectural practices. In selecting RPBW, they were able to ensure that there was collaboration on all aspects of the design and construction of Aurora Place. It was from the developers own architectural group, Lend Lease Design Group (LLDG), that much of the *genius loci* was synthesized together with an understanding of existing city places, such as Farrer, Chifley and Macquarie. LLDG worked as architects in association to design, develop and document the building. RPBW took responsibility for the 'skins' [façade, wind and environmental engineering] and LLDG took the main responsibility for the core and the 'frame' [civil, structural engineering] and the systems [services, transport and IT engineering]. From an early stage all project documentation was installed progressively on Project Web, an internet publication application developed by Lend Lease. The system provided a general availability of all drawings from a multitude of sources across the internet. This enabled what was in effect a 24 hour Genoa/Sydney office with drawing issue as easy as Email—far better than the slower process of FTP transfer of drawings. Close contact between the two offices began at the project's inception when an LLDG team went to Genoa for briefing and workshops. It was at these workshops that the design concept was developed. From that point on RPBW partners made frequent visits to Sydney in addition to those made by Renzo Piano himself.

This design dialogue was fortunately a process which LLDG had used on many other projects and thus married well with the RPBW methodology.[12]

In all of this there was nothing inconsistent with the Building Workshop's idea of process. For them working with another architectural team is part of consultation and the collaboration part of Piano's objective to reacquire the design process. Working this way, in team format on large projects continually consulting and listening is exhaustive and exhausting. From the Building Workshop's point of view the process is an obvious and logical way to discharge the architectural responsibility they take seriously, viewed from the outside the process itself is an important characteristic that distinguishes them.

[1] Renzo Piano interviewed by V.M.Lampugnani, *Domus* No 688, p.20.

[2] Buchanan, P [1999] *Renzo Piano Building Workshop Vol 1*, p.35.

[4] Ibid *Domus* 688.

[5] Ibid *Domus* 688.

[6] Frampton, K [1996] *Studies in Tectonic Culture*, p.386.

[7] Ibid *Domus* 688.

[8] Ibid *Domus* 688.

[19] Ibid *Domus* and Buchanan Vol 1.

[10] See: Renzo Piano Building Workshop 1964/1991: In Search of a Balance *Process Architecture No 700*, quoted in *Frampton, Studies in Tectonic Culture*, p383.

[12] Dyshart, B [1998] the *Digital Document*.

[12] Conversation with Ross Bonthorne, Principal Architect, LLDG 5/02/01.

Logistical Web

Design complexity, geographic separation and ambiguous competing interests are some of the constant dilemmas in a high profile international design project.

In response to these problems, Lend Lease built a web-based collaboration system that provided a secure, controlled access point for all project participants to share project information from anywhere in the world. It was an ambitious plan pulled together with the belief that a project of this stature was going to require innovation on all fronts, including its use of information technology.

It was ambitious in that it was attempting to address the juxtaposition between the tactile, craft-based approach of the Renzo Piano Building Workshop, the incessantly paper-based culture of most project managers and the perceived complexity of computing technology in a traditionally conservative industry. The core issue was to solve the problem of how to communicate globally on design progress and documentation status in the most timely manner possible. The most obvious answer was to utilise the rapidly emerging popularity of the Internet as a part of the solution.

What evolved was a system called ProjectWeb whereby project managers, consultants, subcontractors and suppliers could all gain secure access to a common set of documents. These might be drawings, digital photos, memorandums, requests for information, site instructions and many other forms of documentation. When using ProjectWeb it was possible to transmit digital images of the large wooden 1:1 models stored in Genoa, provide instant access to concept plans to a development manager's office or publish progress reports and programs to the site team from anywhere in the world.

Getting such a plan off the ground was no easy feat and at one stage the whole project was almost put aside, being perceived as a major distraction due to the required changes in workplace behaviour. One day when a meeting was scheduled to consider the Project Web proposal, the chief executive stared at his computer screen and asked why the figures he was seeing there were more up-to-date than those in a report that had taken weeks to prepare manually. It was a forceful message about how communication using networked computers was more immediate and beneficial than paper. Even more importantly, the most senior person in Lend Lease knew how to access the information!

From this point onwards, the system continued its development and implementation, eventually rolling out to many other projects. Today, the ProjectWeb application has evolved within Lend Lease to the point where it now supports over $7 billion worth of projects with over 7700 participants across 15 countries. A success story initiated by the compelling need to push the boundaries of technical innovation on every front.

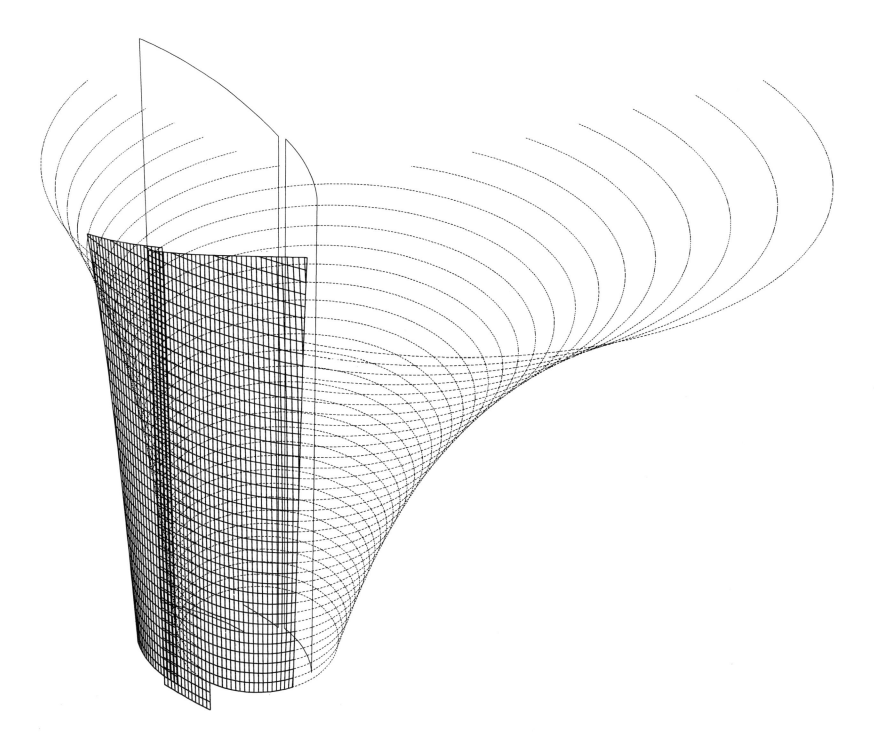

SOUTH EAST GEOMETRY

Architectural Analysis

OPPOSITE The western facade of the commercial tower with the northwest fin gleaming in the afternoon sunlight.

In cityscapes like Sydney, constructed relatively recently, the form is already dictated by the skyscraper program. Skyscrapers are, by their very nature, self-contained, arrogant and domineering. In order to avoid such perverse logic and have the building profit from the sun and the climatic conditions of the area, we decided to soften it's forms, to design them for the wind and not against it.[1]

The 43 floor commercial building and the adjacent 16 floor apartment building which comprise Aurora place are, as Piano himself puts it ...a homage to the city.'[2] In so doing it addresses the banality of the skyscraper typology and refers to the sublime marine environment of the harbour that readily characterises the city of the 2000 Olympics.

The Aurora Place project demonstrates, that no matter how tried, true and hackneyed the contemporary commercial office tower and apartment building may seem, it is always possible—indeed emphatically worthwhile—to go back to first principles and proceed with rigour. To do this one must be prepared to ask

obvious, fundamental questions and then to assess the likely glib '...it can't be done' responses systematically and empirically. For example, working on the Sydney tower RPBW obviously asked: why do all office buildings have to be hermetically sealed and air-conditioned? Why is there no social and spatial modulation of spaces within such a building and why does every floor have to be identical, or to put that another way: why must a skyscraper's form be so uniform?

Chifley Tower [Kohn, Pederson Fox architects, 1988] and Governor Phillip Tower [Denton, Corker Marshall architects, 1994], the two neighbours which 'bookend' the Aurora Place tower, provide interesting object lessons in the architectural form of the tall tower block. The 1988 building presents itself to the passer-by as a collection of architectural quotations from the history of the 20th century skyscraper, whereas the 1994 tower coolly accepts uniformity as a virtue and elevates it to a highbrow aesthetic.

BELOW LEFT A view showing the proximity of the commercial tower (left) and the residential building (right) under construction. BELOW View of the SW corner of the building featuring the west sail, stepped facade and the 'fishscale' (leaning) facade. RIGHT PAGE This plan gives a perfect view of the buildings on the site and their relationship to Bent and Phillip streets.

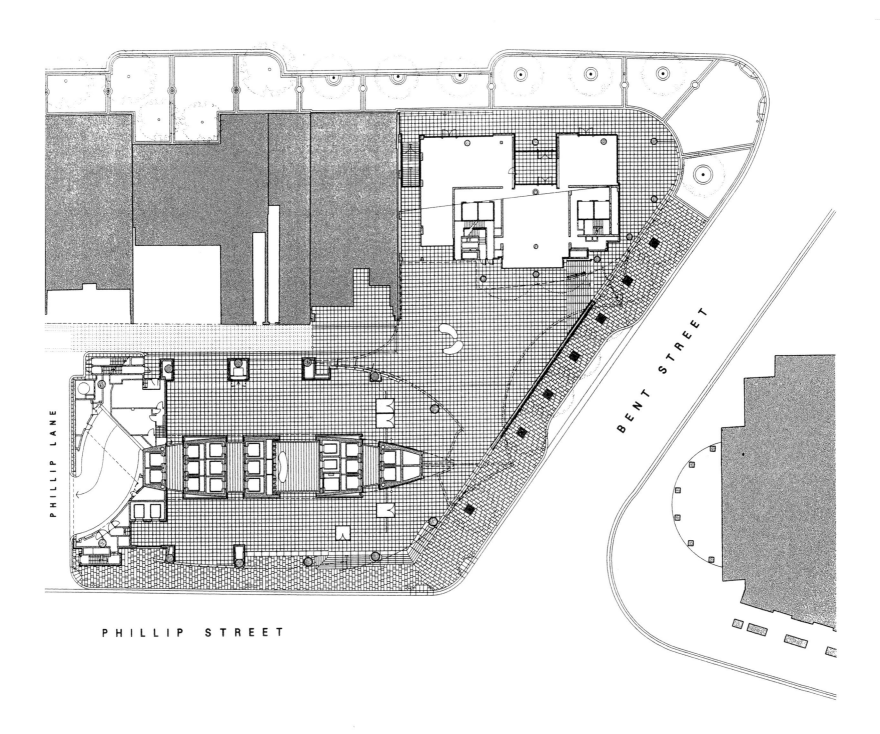

PHILLIP LANE

BENT STREET

PHILLIP STREET

ABOVE After detachment, the grillage is swung away and dismantled at ground carrying level. OPPOSITE Riggers are seen here detaching the grillage from the jump form to the core node high above the city.

In Sydney it is also true that other architects have asked these worthwhile questions and proceeded along similar lines. However Piano, perhaps because he has come to the skyscraper as an architect with all the confidence of maturity and a convincing record of inventive eclecticism, adopted a very different emphasis in the formulation of his skyscraper stratagem. Amongst other things, he has attempted a social modulation of spaces and he has attempted a figurative dematerialising, or 'detachment' of the tower's glass facades. Put simply, he has provided outdoor social spaces on each floor to ameliorate the workplace monoculture that is the contemporary high-rise office building, and he has designed a tower façade which is much more than a mere see-through raincoat to the building. The tower facade achieves a sculptural complexity that is over and above the bottom line specification for the exterior wall of a building. In fact this new skyscraper stratagem in Sydney is an integrated one: the architectural delivery of both these innovations are interdependent on one another and connected to other attributes that give the buildings their particular qualities.

However, before proceeding to more detail we should note that the Piano stratagem goes beyond these two architectural and social moves. The idea of social space also exists in the ground floor and street level regions of the apartment and office buildings standing together on the corner of Macquarie, Bent and Phillip Streets in Sydney. There are several aspects to this. Firstly, the idea of constructing a podium to the tower, or even both buildings was rejected in favour of a simple, open piazza. Then, the visual impact of the two buildings was reduced as far as possible, in particular the façade of the large office tower was made transparent at the ground level. The idea is to make invisible—

or approach—invisibility; Piano calls it dematerialising. The effect is to offer the visitor a clear view into the building's lobby with minimal visual distraction. A green 'Austral Verde' granite flows seamlessly through all of the interior and exterior piazza spaces with the sill framing for the glass sheets of the lobby walls recessed out of sight beneath its surface. The use of this material was intended to 'stitch' the building back into the urban fabric.

Next, the site's major historic connections have impinged on the design of the ground plane. If, in other projects, Piano treats the site as landscape[3] or reads it as nature, at Aurora Place the manoeuvre is to treat the site as a fragment of the city with all its historical connections intact. Thus the site opens up to established pedestrian routes like Phillip Lane, and is easily entered from the Bent and Phillip Street edges. In this regard though there is clearly some tension between the apartment residents' need for privacy and the openness of the piazza on which their building sits. For this reason the residential lobby hasn't had quite the same dematerialising treatment as the Aurora Place office tower. Therefore the flow of pedestrian traffic through it to Macquarie Street may well be diminished, which would be unfortunate. To help offset this possibility, not only is the ground plane treated consistently across the entire site, but also a suspended glass canopy links the two towers to roof-in the piazza and effectively creates a sense of cover. In the absence of this simple device it would have been difficult to create a sense of enclosure at ground level. The practical consequence of roofing the piazza in this way is to offer the user or passer-by some respite from Sydney's frequent heavy rain showers and the inevitable powerful down-draught winds coming off the sheer glass surfaces of the two towers.

44 Architectural Analysis

Like other architectural products the suspended glass canopy has a lineage that begins in earlier Building Workshop endeavours. In this case the Banca Popolare di Lodi headquarters building project in Italy than ran from 1991–98[4], contained the Workshop's first use of the suspended glass and steel roof assemblage. Like Aurora Place, it was used to provide an external social space and to harmonise the space between buildings of diverse form which shared the same site.

Other aspects of the Aurora Place commercial tower lobby arise from Piano's concern for the experiential in architecture and invoke comment. To extend the effect of transparency over the full day/night cycle, the lobby lighting has been designed with strong up-lighters so that the lobby ceiling inside and the suspended canopy outside appear as one after dark. Relieving the lobby walls of their normal function of demarcation beween interior and exterior also raises the problem of how to impart a sense of arrival, of entry, to the office tower at street level. At Aurora Place this happens not at the tall, glass lobby walls but at the point one reaches the actual lift lobbies in the building's core. In contrast to the outer lobby's grand scale, these spaces are more intimate and the material palette suddenly switches from stone to wood. Tasmanian Oak lining boards are placed with minimal joints on the floor and walls, while the ceiling is lined with timber veneered panels. In these smaller spaces the acoustics are less brittle and the lighting softer; the contrast with the world outside is obvious and you then feel you have entered the building.

Noting all of this and accepting the level of finesse that is reached, we must also examine RPBW's use of terracotta before discussing the towers proper. For Piano,

terracotta is more than a mere material: it is a cladding and walling system that is both a metaphor for the earth itself and a contextualising instrument. Over the years Piano and his team team have invested this material with a quantum of techno-scientific thought and painstaking consideration of production that is normally found only in industrial design. With his terracotta technology Piano has developed a technique of assembly which, in turn, has become a technique of architectural composition that manifests itself as a major presence in the architectural works. The Sydney project is the seventh where this ancient walling system has been used by the Workshop. Their terracotta sequence starts with three French projects going back to the 1988–89 IRCAM extension in Paris. Here, the 'discovery' of terracotta facing was made in circumstances driven by a need for Piano to assuage the insertion of a contemporary building into a sensitive historical context. It worked, and was quickly followed by the Rue de Meaux Housing [1988–91] in Paris where the terracotta assemblies were integrated with glass reinforced cement framing and louvres. Next came the Cité International de Lyon [1986–95] where terracotta is used in conjunction with the 'thermal cushion' louvred glass wall that also appears on the Sydney apartment building. Terracotta was also used in parts of the Genoa Columbus International Exposition project of 1984–92 and, most extensively, at Potsdamer Platz in Berlin [1992–99].

In Sydney terracotta cladding is used as an exterior material in a balanced composition along with curtain wall and glass elements. It is also used as the material of the wintergarden spaces in Aurora Place to suggest exteriority; it is used as an agency of mediation with the surrounding historical city and it is used to 'ground' both the buildings to suggest that they grow out of the site.

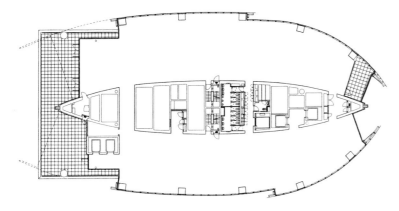

Low Rise Level 6 Plan

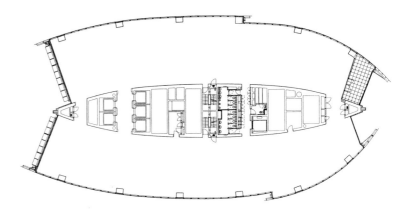

Typical Low Rise Plan

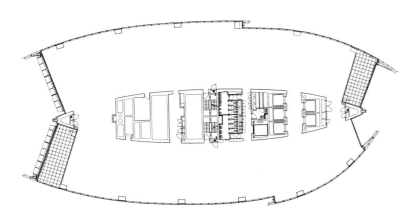

Typical Mid Rise Plan

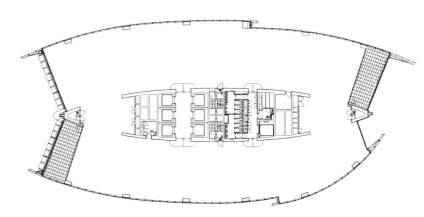

Typical High Rise Plan

Architectural Analysis

The nature of how this soaring, sculptural tower grows out of the surrounding cityscape is in fact a unique quality of the Piano design. This cityscape is Piano's description of the carefully composed massive terracotta clad rectilinear elements at the base of the buildings. The choice of terracotta here is important as it not only reflects the materials used in the existing streetscape, but also creates a human, earthy texture to the buildings at ground level.[5]

One of the significant accomplishments of the Aurora Place project is the manner in which these terracotta forms are skilfully manipulated to construct a set of intricate relationships to the diverse architectural context that surrounds the site, and in the case of the northern boundaries, actually abuts the site. The colour and texture of the terracotta and its flexible plasticity help to make this possible, but it is the perceptiveness of the architectural approach here that is impressive. Within the pedestrian's gaze a series of two, three, four and five storey forms present themselves at every turn to give a warm, tactile masonry-like visual field that almost naturally takes on an archaeological quality.

In the buildings themselves terracotta has a threefold presence: as a solid cladding [with 'shadow grooves'] on the facades; as a fine batten screen to mask mechanical grilles and for privacy on the residential apartments; and as a smooth, curved cladding to the columns. On both buildings, terracotta provides a contrast to the white fritted glass in different ways. Aurora Place is mostly smooth white glass, but a measure of terracotta persists as lining to the tower wintergardens, stretching all the way up the building on the narrow north and south elevations. In this way the terracotta matches the scale of the city as well as that of the neighbourhood. The solid red base to the buildings is one of the parallels with Utzon's Sydney Opera House where there is a similar tectonic layer of heavy red-brown base surmounted by a light white superstructure. On the apartment building terracotta is harnessed to represent human scale and is therefore more obvious right through the base of the building and up the eastern façade, wrapping around the south east corner of Bent and Macquarie Streets. Here the amplitude of panels and joints in walling, window openings and louvres is an authoritative demonstration of the system's aesthetic flexibility and the architect's craft in the use of it.

An examination of the typical office floor plan shows how the long east walls of the tower are curved to mould the floor plate wider in the middle and narrower at each end making the building very broad. Two well known antecedents are Gio Ponti's 1958 Pirelli Building in Milan and the 1963 Pan Am Building in New York, designed by Walter Gropius and Pietro Belluschi with Emery Roth and Sons. Although both these examples have faceted rather than curved facades, they represent a skyscraper form that repays study. The office tower at Aurora Place, however, is a more complex form both in its façade architecture and especially in its top or crown.

Whilst there is a pragmatic logic to using large areas of glass in an office tower, such as giving the building visual coherence and making optimal use of available daylight, glass in the tower building at Aurora Place is also an important material on the agenda for architectural expression. *(continued on page 58)*

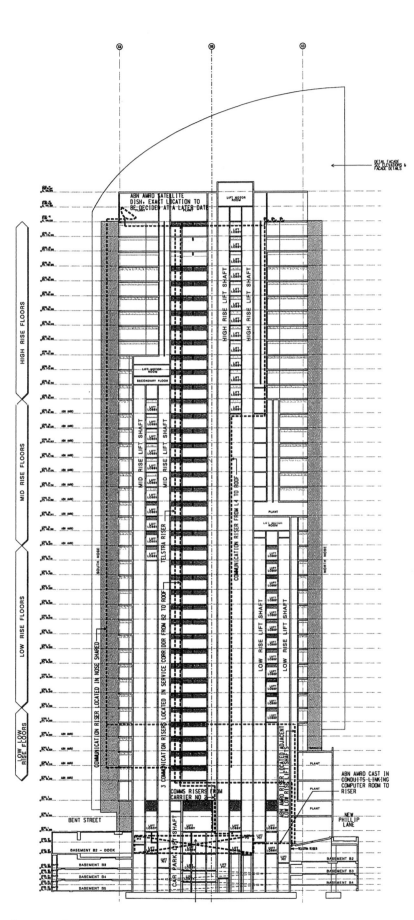

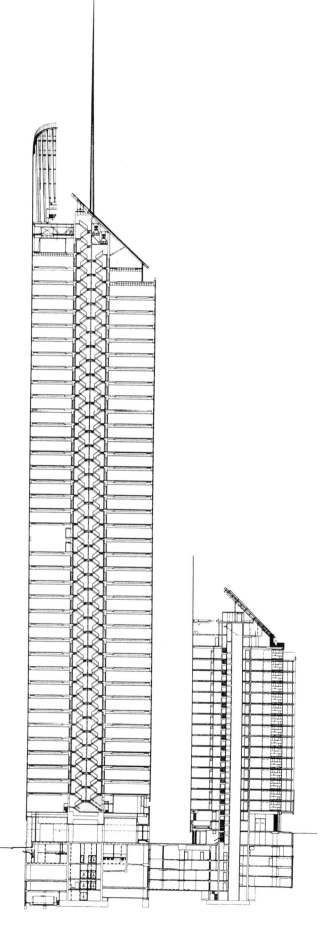

SCHEMATIC SECTION LOOKING WEST

SCHEMATIC SECTION LOOKING NORTH

Structural Framing

The structural elements of the tower building can be considered as two components; the primary building frame, and the secondary structural facade support elements attached to the building frame.

The primary building frame is constructed from reinforced and post-tensioned concrete and the secondary structural elements are constructed from structural steel and interact directly with the external facade components.

The core and the frame action of the slabs and tower columns contribute to the lateral stability of the building. This requires that the floor-core connection be designed to resist the applied frame moments. Each floor acts as a mini-outrigger eliminating the need to adopt a centralised floor-to-floor outrigger system that would occupy valuable space within the building.

A 320mm thickened slab around the core enhances the floor-core moment connection and screwed couplers provide a continuous connection for the thickened slab to the core.

The core provides 70% of the lateral load stiffness and the remaining 30% is taken by the combined frame action of the slabs and tower columns.

The reinforced concrete core has a maximum width of 9.5m. The floor slabs span each side of the core 10.8m and 12.0m to the perimeter beams. Six tower columns, spaced at 10.8m centres, support the floors each side of the core and are located along the curved east and west building perimeter. The floor plates cantilever at the four corners of the structure. The SE corner of the tower structure gradually extends and leans eastward at every level, resulting in a 5.0m change in span

of the edge beam between Level 3 and Level 41.

Notched post-tensioned band beams between the core and the perimeter beams have been designed to a minimum depth to optimise services clearances and are typically 470mm deep and 600mm wide. The floor beams are spaced at 2.7m centres and support a 120mm-thick reinforced concrete floor plate. The floor to floor height is typically 3.72m. Perimeter edge beams are 880mm deep x 400mm wide and cantilever northwards and southwards to support the wintergardens and projecting facade elements. The edge beams and facade elements (fins) cantilever in excess of 10m beyond the first internal column.

Specified concrete strengths for the project varied between 80MPa and 32MPa. High performance concrete was used to control long-term differential axial shortening,

shrinkage and creep between the columns and core walls.

The four basement levels extend out to the perimeter of the site. The construction of the tower columns and level 3 floor plate was accelerated from the foundations utilising composite structural steel framing. The reinforced tubular column forms were pumped with high strength concrete from their base up to a height of 25 metres.

Base fixity of the core structure is provided by a 1.5m thick core raft permanently anchored into the bedrock. Along the perimeter of the outer core walls, ten permanent rock anchors each of 8000kN capacity are drilled through the core raft approximately 16m into the sandstone bedrock.

The cantilevered sail needles that project above plant Level 44 are restrained by composite structural steel floor systems incorporated in the two top levels of the tower.

OPPOSITE The core structure is seen on the left with the jump form at level 20. Note the needle erection of the residential sail on the right of the picture. TOP CENTRE The installation of a needle for the west sail on the roof of the commercial building. BOTTOM CENTRE A concrete pour takes place at one of the higher levels. BELOW LEFT The start of the structural steel installation on the roof. FOLLOWING PAGES The mast is 99m in height and made up in three sections. The top section (the needle) measures 18m and includes a chain damper to reduce sway in high wind. A rigger is waiting on a platform inside the second section ready to attach an internal bolting ring.

56 Architectural Analysis

The milky white fritted glass curtain walls that sheathe the east and west facades consist of open jointed panellized glazing fixed with structural silicone. The white colour is achieved by the use of a single laminated and white fritted pane of low-iron glass throughout the whole installation. On the large vision panels the frit fades to create a clear vision window. Overall, a delicate white patterned façade gives the tower its special quality. For Renzo Piano the operative visual metaphor for the tower facades is that of a sail, but it is not a sail that is limited to the contour of the tower itself. In fact the façade carries well past the ends of the building and cantilevers into space at each end [described by Piano as fins], and is discontinuous across the whole façade with a distinct vertical break, or step, in the middle where the outer façade is made to overlap the inner one. If it is a sail it is unfurling and if it is a building it is de-laminating and decomposing in an uncanny sort of way for such a large object. The compositional technique aligns with Piano's concept of de-materialising, but is used here on a hitherto unattempted scale except perhaps for the Debis tower in Berlin. Whatever the metaphor, the effect is striking and unlike anything else in the city.

However the loftiest metaphor at Aurora Place derives from Piano's respect for the shell roof forms of Jorn Utzon's Sydney Opera House [1956–73] which is less than a kilometre away at the bottom of Macquarie Street. In designing the tops to his buildings, Piano, who refers to the Opera House as Sydney's trademark and has spoken of paying 'homage to Sydney' and how '...a dialogue between the two buildings is inevitable,' has projected both building's west façades upward, to fill a soaring profile reminiscent of the Opera House silhouette. The metallic louvred roofs of the two buildings are then canted back at an angle of 43 degrees to rest against these curving projections. Then the wall projections continue up further still, beyond the envelope of the building itself, separating the wall from the building below. With the western sun behind it, the free standing, curved glass wall achieves Piano's intention of making it appear like a sail fully loaded with wind.

Just as we can read Piano's piazza as 'nature' then, in a similar way, we can see the office floors as a kind of interior 'nature' or 'internal landscape.'[7] Inside the office tower, the effect of the curving facades on the typical office floors is to create a sweeping feeling of space. The business side of this office building then consists of two 10–12 metre wide bands of column-free space either side of a solid core that is built on the same gently curving arc as the facades. These bands of office space lead to the wintergardens—protected by the façade 'fins'—at the north and south ends. This office space is inspiringly open and flexible and represents an opportunity for interior design. It lends itself to open plan, non cellular types of layout and actually challenges the occupants to find new ways of working. For example, adopting open planning, developed around management organisational strategies such as task teams, in place of the orthodoxy of a department based cellular office layout with individual offices and connecting corridors.[8]

In a related gesture the RPBW has also rejected cellular compartments in favour of open plan living in the residential apartment plans. Although bedroom privacy implies cell-like rooms, even these have been moderated with retractable screens where adjoining rooms abut exterior walls.

With living, kitchen and dining spaces open planned, and expansive balconies facing Macquarie Street to the east, spatial continuity is assured, particularly as all apartments have external windows on the west to the east facades to take advantage of cross ventilation. (continued on page 76)

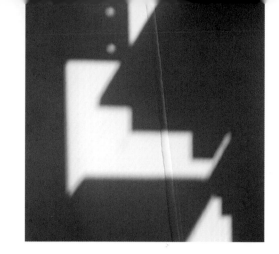

Geometry

The geometry of the office tower at Aurora Place in plan is straightforward being based on a simple faceted cylindrical geometry which maximises repetition in the glazing panels in most areas.

The shape of the southern part of the eastern facade changes slightly on every floor, thus making the facade sweep out dramatically. This flaring form, part of a cone, has been generated by the use of diminishing radii at each floor, from the top down.

The significant advantage of this twisting form is that it not only produces increased floor areas in the top of the office building where space is more valuable, but it also increases the size of the public piazza at the base of the buildings.

The extensions of the facades beyond the enclosure of the tower building are called 'fins' and 'sails'.

These glass facades are gently curving and continuous from street level to the top (sail) and to the extremities in plan (fins).

Trimmed like sails on a yacht, the fins and sails serve to lessen the effects of wind, sun and rain on the facade and on the ground plane.

The oblique cut at the top was determined by a 'sun-access plane', to prevent undue overshadowing of the Royal Botanic Gardens opposite Aurora Place.

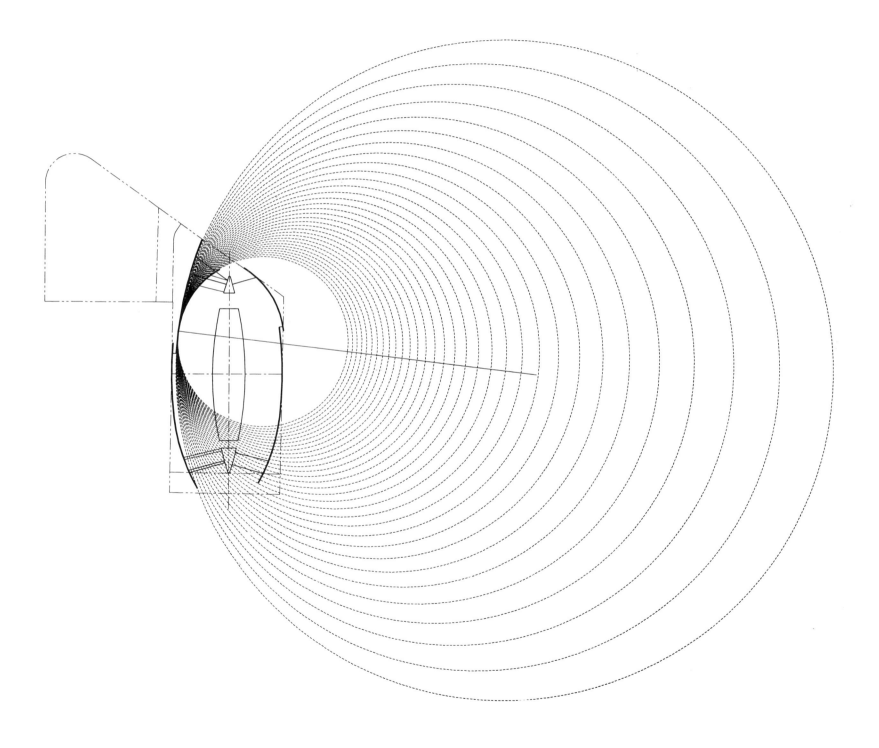

FLOOR GEOMETRY DIAGRAM

Ground Plane

Unlike contemporary podium based buildings which effectively separate and obscure the identity of the tower from the street, the identifiable shape of this unfurling flower-like form is immediately evident from the ground. There is a direct relationship between Aurora Place's urban identity and its human scale, with the facade of the tower coming right down to the street. The rejection of the podium has freed the ground plane around the buildings, creating an important interactive, social space for people both day and night.

The nature of how this soaring sculptural tower grows out of the surrounding cityscape is in fact a unique quality of the design. The choice of terracotta here is important as it not only reflects the materials used in the existing streetscape, but also creates a human, earthy texture to the buildings at ground level.

In the same manner a continuity of granite paving throughout the commercial tower lobby and piazza of Aurora Place links the internal and external ground plane of the development and that of surrounding buildings. Aligned with the orthogonal city geometry, the colour, texture and form blend the buildings into their context.

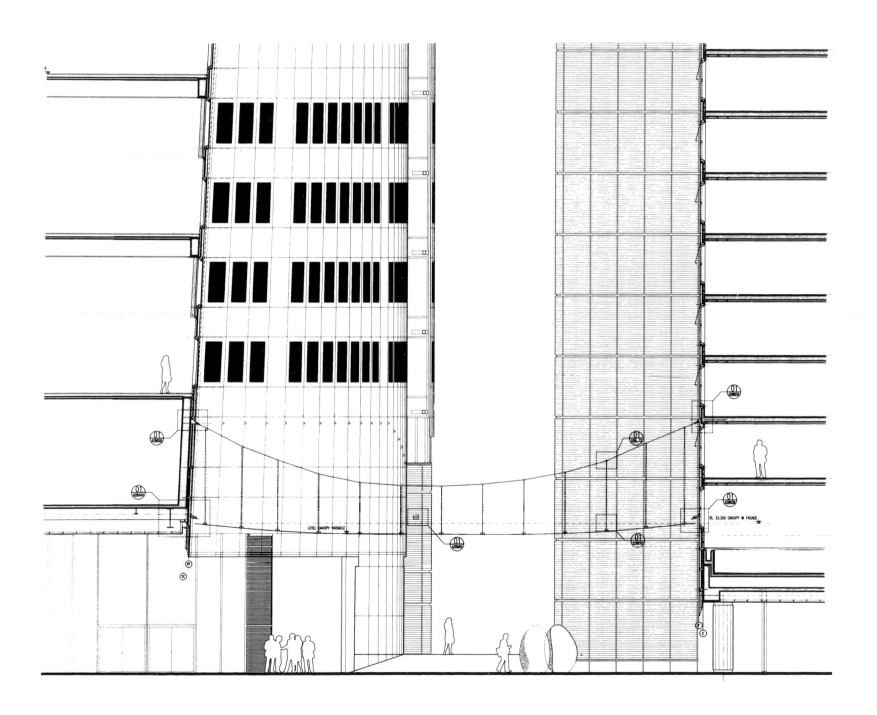

EAST WEST CANOPY SECTION

Wintergardens

Adding a new dimension to the way office towers are perceived, the natural environment of the wintergardens demonstrates that the skyscraper doesn't have to be a hermetically sealed building. Located in the NW and SE corners of the tower floor plate and maximising the dramatic harbour and park views these wintergardens are occupiable balconies elaborated with a sophisticated operable louvre facade. They allow a unique and direct interface with Sydney's temperate climate. With single and double storey volumes, depending on their location in the tower building, and on every level in the residential building, the wintergardens provide an exciting, naturally ventilated respite that mediates between the external and internal environments.

Beyond the inner glass membrane of the tower building, the wintergardens have been conceived as a social space, a break-out

space, a garden, and a place to get away from the office.

These stimulating wintergarden spaces are defined by the four different textures or surfaces of the building. The fritted dematerialising skin of the fins, the terracotta core, a full height glass wall with fixed and louvred panels, and finally the glass interface with the office environment.

The floor is an impervious external finish and in keeping with the external fabric of the building the moisture resistant ceiling is painted a warm white. All services including indirect lighting are also weather resistant.

Each occupant can adjust their louvres and blinds according to the time of day or season. It is a working facade where each of the pieces is not only in full view, but there to be appreciated.

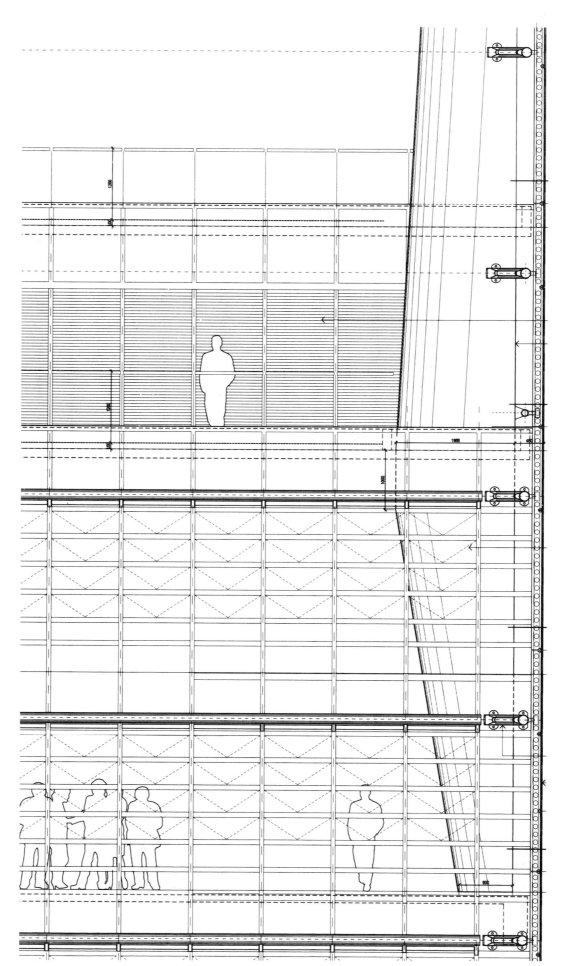

WEST FACADE SAIL SECTION

OPPOSITE Typical view of a wintergarden in the residential building looking toward the south east through the glass louvred facade.

Architectural Analysis

To complement these plans the whole of the residential eastern façade is overlain with deep balconies wrapped with glass louvres to create wintergardens, and also to cushion some of the traffic noise from the street below. This enormous glass cage with an ever-changing pattern of operable louvres has antecedents in other Piano residential buildings[9] where its use is also associated with terracotta cladding. In fact the residential building in Sydney is instantly recognisable to followers of Piano's work, although the elements of terracotta and glass cage are developments rather than repetitions of previous designs.[10] Perhaps Renzo Piano was alluding to this and to the associative impact of everyday materials like glass and terracotta on our collective memories when he said: '...eternity is not achieved by building in stone, rather it is established by repeating gestures that are the same.'[11]

When all of these things are considered the real achievement is the integrative approach to the architectural task. That is to say the conceptual circularity of all the constituent ideas—how each one connects to the next to form a comprehensive tactical suite of rules for the project. In turn every part of the architectural project is organised and executed in complete consistency with the specific rules and how the architectural work is then completed with maximum technical and expressive economy. Any number of examples will serve to illustrate this point but just one set of connected 'rules' will do. The façades, for example, do not just 'de - materialise' or entertain the metaphor of a sail for the sake of it. The curved glass surfaces contribute to softening the effect of wind on the building, they condition the interior space and character of the offices, they cantilever past the volume of the building to provide shelter to the wintergardens of the office tower and they

extend up to form the crown of the buildings. The wintergardens in their turn enrich the social life of each floor, the terracotta lining in them tracks down the building to the piazza which is another social space that also respects the site's linkages into the rest of the city. The symbol of the city is an Opera House that carries the metaphor of the sail and so on. Clearly this level of inter-connectivity of parts is not coincidental but strategic—it's as if an idea or a technique only makes the grade if it is embracing in the functional, metaphorical and technical senses and has the potential to make linkages across the project. To be sure this is not unique to RPBW but precious few do it as well and with such intentionality and precision.

1   Renzo Piano interview in Anatxu. Zabalbeascoa [1998] *Renzo Piano; Sustainable Architectures* p59.
2   Renzo Piano [1997] *Renzo Piano Logbook* p242.
3   Paolo Tombesi, 'Contextual Piano' in *UME* No9. Pp46–7.
4   Peter Buchanan ed. [2000] *Renzo Piano Building workshop; Complete Works, Volume Four pp 136–154.*
5   Renzo Piano Building Workshop [2000] *Aurora Place.*
7   Renzo Piano Building Workshop [2000] *Aurora Place* p7.
8   Lend Lease Corporation and the East Asia Property Group [nd] *Aurora Place* p43.
9   Particulalry the Paris, Lyon and Berlin projects that are mentioned elsewhere. See Peter Buchanan Ed. [1993–2000] *Renzo Piano Building Workshop; Complete Works, Vol. 4.*
11 Renzo Piano, 'Piece by Piece' ABC-TV Documentary, screened 3/9/00

Residential Building

The apartment building sits within the existing scale of Macquarie Street, an historically important residential address. The entrance to the apartments is flanked with shops on the ground floor and a swimming pool and fitness studio is located on the mezzanine. Most apparent is the kinetic glass louvre facade which provides a changing kaleidoscope of city living.

The apartments run the full depth of the building linking occupants by a wide gallery from the Royal Botanic Gardens-side, to the Piazza where the mainly sleeping areas are protected by curved shell-like, fritted glass facades.

The louvred glass façade of the apartment building has been conceived as kinetic crystalline sculpture, draped across the balconies of the apartments to create wintergardens. This shelters the balconies from rain and wind and so extends the periods when they can be used.

The east side of the apartment opens in a series of layers to suspend the occupants in their own 'botanic garden greenhouse'. The layers of sliding glass, opaque terracotta battens, motorised blinds and entirely low-iron glass with operable louvres, allow the user to engage with or retreat from the view and climate as mood and comfort require. The terracotta cladding fits protectively 'like a jacket' over the building.

The highest floors are occupied by penthouses, having a roofgarden with spectacular views, protected from the wind by the 'sail' and from the sun by operable louvres.

BELOW AND OPPOSITE Several views of the reception area of the residential building on Macquarie Street.

BELOW LEFT A swimming pool is located on the mezzanine level of the residential building. BELOW AND RIGHT Several views of a typical apartment showing bedroom and kitchen areas.

FOLLOWING PAGE View of the living area of an apartment looking through to its wintergarden and on to the Royal Botanic Gardens. The room can be expanded to become one large space.

76

Technology

OPPOSITE The casting process for one of the 'football' nodes which are used to hold up the glazed canopy over the piazza.

Architects make use of the tools that their time offers them.[1]
Architecture is born of its own time and has to be capable of expressing this.[2]

Technology—the intentional bringing to bear of rational thought upon the world of objects —is a central theme in modern architecture where it is better described as the bringing to bear of not only rational, but of poetic thought to building construction. Until quite recently technology in architecture was little discussed outside of the stylistic discourse on hi-tech architecture where the theoretical development of ideas was often far less advanced than their design expression.

In the sense that his architecture is a precise, craftsman-like assemblage of constituent elements carefully fabricated in response to real world needs, Renzo Piano is, as he puts it, a *homo faber* in the Renaissance sense of the term.[3] *Homo faber*, perhaps, 'he who makes' also refers in a broad sense to a 'metalworker or fabricator' [in the 15th century leading scientists/inventors such as Gutenberg and Brunelleschi were trained as metalworkers]. Piano consistently differentiates between

himself and other architects characterising his activity as a kind of scientific building. He has aspired also to the model of the 16th century *machinatore*, or designer/inventor who not only designs but controls the means of production. Piano's self-classification as a builder rather than an architect asks us to consider that, at its most poetic, building is architecture. A study of the work of a creative 'fabricator' thus entails a consideration of technology.

During the last decade, in response to the extensive range of techno-morphological solutions engendered through the 20th century, a new stream of architectural critique has developed around what might be called the art of building construction. Publications such as Kenneth Frampton's *Studies in Tectonic Culture*, 1996 and Gevork Hartoonian's *Ontology of Construction*, 1994 have introduced 'fabrication' and 'tectonics' into the discourse on contemporary architectural theory and practice. Accepting these contributions, the aim of this chapter is quickly to contextualise the discussion of technology outside the disciplinary framework of architecture before returning to the work of Renzo Piano, *homo faber*.

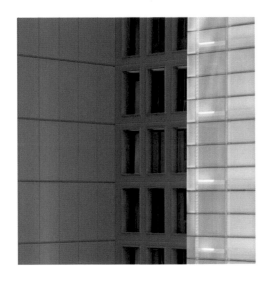

Above The framed reveal of the 'Juliet' balconies are reflected in the glass of the westen facade of the wintergardens of the residential building.
Opposite Page The view from the piazza looking up at the 'Juliet' balconies to the roof exhaust stacks and to the rail at the top of the residential building. Following Pages Looking up through the partly completed canopy.

A century ago we wouldn't have been discussing the poesy of building or celebrating the art of the fabricator. However, there is a technical aspect to architecture today that didn't exist then and at the close of the 19th century there was a particular visual furnishing role for architecture that doesn't exist today. We can see this virtual inversion of meaning in John Ruskin declaiming that architecture is '...the art which so disposes and adorns the edifices raised by man, for whatever uses, that the sight of them may contribute to his mental health, power and pleasure...' He immediately goes on to make a distinction between architecture and building which doesn't apply in quite the same way today, saying that to build is '...to put together and adjust the several pieces of any edifice or receptacle of a considerable size'.[4] Ruskin cited a church, a house, a ship and a coach building as examples of this art of building or 'edification' as he called it. Merely to construct something is not architecture, he said, but building. The term architecture applies, Ruskin contended, when one '...impresses on its form certain characters venerable or beautiful, but otherwise unnecessary.' Technology had no real place in Ruskin's world-view, however he did express the idea that, in architecture, there needs to be an intrinsic relationship between ornament and structure. His contemporary Viollet-le-Duc argued for the appearance of a building to reflect its construction. In fact Gevork believes these dictums are different expressions of the same idea.[5]

During the 20th century a more general discourse on technology and society emerged, revolving around positive and negative views on the influence of technology in advanced capitalist societies. According to the two positions, technology is either a neutral means that enables the realisation of purposeful, rational ends or it is an ideologically driven, dystopian presence that ineluctably manipulates human existence. The first view, that of technology as a positive instrument, is associated with Jurgen Habermas and Marshall Sahlins[6] and would also seem to be the view of Renzo Piano:

I find the distrust of advanced technology still more ludicrous, especially when it culminates in the fiercely academic tones used in the condemnation or acclaim of high technology. Architects should work with the tools that their time offers them. Refusing to deal with contemporary material culture is totally futile, perhaps even a bit masochistic. Let us put it this way: technology is like a bus. If it helps you to get where you want to go you take it. If its going in a different direction, don't.[7]

Perhaps Piano's talk of '...academic tones used in condemnation...' may be a reference to the German philosopher Martin Heidegger who is the better known protagonist of the second, or negative view of technology. In his 1954 essay 'The Question Concerning Technology', Heidegger begins with a stricture warning us to be wary of the common view that we control technology, in fact he says '...we remain unfree and chained to technology'. Further, we are actually 'delivered over to technology in the worst possible way, if we regard it as something neutral.'[8] Writing shortly after World War II, Heidegger worried about the potential for humankind to be enframed by technology and reduced to a sort of on-call human stockpile for technological purposes. His influential and widely read essay also explores the meaning of the word technology, tracing it to the Greek *technikon* meaning that which belongs to *techne*.

With direct relevance to Renzo Piano and the *fabricatore* theme, Heidegger then makes two observations about the word *techne*. First, the word is applicable not only to the talents and skills of the craftsman but also to the world of the intellect and of the fine arts. Secondly, Heidegger says '*techne* belongs to the bringing—forth, to poesis; it is something poetic.'[9]

Hartoonian enters the discussion on Heidegger's 'The Question Concerning Technology' and calls *techne* '...the art of making', that not only privileges craftmanship and fabrication, but assigns them a cultural value that recognises the presence of intellectual capital. Thus the difference between *techne* and technology is that the latter '...draws only from its own reserves of physics and mechanics—while techne precedes practical knowledge and resides, in part, in poetics.'[10]

At Aurora Place, RPBW's use of *techne* and mastery of technological building production is highly significant. The separate elements of the building are given a precise tectonic form based on their place and fit in the constructional assemblage. In this way a tectonic ordering system derived from a part's relationships with others and with the whole. For example the curtain wall 'sails and fins' have architectural forms derived from a constant interplay of technology and constraint, specifically between the glass sheets and their skeletal steel support, moving from the visually substantial to the visually light. A gradual 'dematerialising: of the glazing occurs where cantilevered structural framing is pushed to the limit of lightness and visually reduces or feathers off towards the extreme edges with ever decreasing means of support. This continues until there is nothing left at the outer edge of the assemblage except a naked sheet of glass hanging in space. Elsewhere, the glass canopy slung between the two buildings speaks of structural support and glass so logically and clearly, as to barely register that there is actually a web-like metal structure doing the seemingly impossible of supporting large sheets of clear glass on a horizontal plane. It is only when you think of the weight of the glass and the thinness of the structural members that you realise how painstakingly developed the whole assemblage is and how precisely the structural and constructional constraints have been creatively used.

Within these and other Building Workshop themes the sense of order is not arbitrary but something which emerges from an interconnected set of rules that govern the parts and the whole. Individual pieces of an assembly conform completely with the rules and the whole work is built with an economy of technical means that is specific to the project and yet thematically connected to a whole set of RPBW precedents. In 1987 Renzo Piano described this technical process this way:

It all makes possible the realisation of an architecture which is an expression of language. This language is examined, invented, and tried out systematically reinventing materials and certain processes, uses or functions, which are coerced or turned inside out. It is not an easy task, but it is the only possible way to try and create a language which is an authentic expression of our century. I am aspiring to the same professional dignity which, perhaps, the architect or designer enjoyed in the 16th century; the architect as *machinatore* who invents and designs something and the instruments to make it and then builds it down to the last detail.[11]

Technology in architecture is palpable technology, not hidden or virtual but rich in formal realities. It is clearly more common to conceal technology in a building than to reveal it, and few of those who do reveal it, do so poetically. The technology that constitutes the figurative aspect of the architecture at Aurora Place is derived from construction, factory production and engineering, three great form-giving agencies of 20th century modernism. In Piano's architecture, technology is pervasive but not randomly or imprecisely used. In Aurora Place, there is a powerful experiential dimension to the presence of technology that, in other hands, could easily be oppressive and dull. In Heideggerian terms Piano's architecture contains a 'bring-forth' not just of technology but of *techne* and poesis, the important knowing that precedes fabrication and the poetry that accompanies it.

Piano believes that architecture is a science that requires courage, and a taste for adventure. He says, to practise architecture one needs to "...tackle reality with curiosity and hope to be able to understand it and change it."[12] Like others,[13] he sees an important sustaining quality in craftmanship, fabrication and science. As well as seeing a noble dimension to the axiomatic truth about the craft nature of architecture he turns his gaze to historical models of the scientist such as Brunelleschi and Galileo the *homo faber* and the *machinatore* for inspiration. For this architect, to make such a broad interpretation of technology is not arbitrary but self-defining. Piano's atavistic appeal to historical models may even reflect a desire to disassociate his contemporary practice from the negative instrumentalism of technology that so troubled Heidegger. Averting our attention to historical models also reminds us of the techno-eschatological dimension to Western culture[14] that goes back at least a thousand years and has

registered a presence in utopian and 'visionary' architecture. In Piano's case this is not to suggest a connection between religion and his architectural vision, but to propose the thought that his work is partially informed by notions of transcendence.

1 Piano, R[1997] *Renzo Piano Logbook*, p.248.

2 *Logbook* p.249.

3 Piano, R[1998] 'The Architect and the President', Pritzker Prize acceptance speech.

4 Ruskin, J [1900] *The Seven Lamps of Architecture*, p.7 Everyman Edition [1940].

5 Hartoonian, G [1994] *Ontology of Construction*, p2.

6 Miller, D [1987] *Material Culture and Mass Consumption*, p.117.

7 *Logbook*, p.248.

8 Heidegger, M [1993], *Basic Writings—The Question Concerning Technology*, p311.

9 *Basic Writings*, p318.

10 *Ontology*, p.40.

11 Lampugnani, VM [1987], Interview with Renzo Piano, *Domus* No 688, p.20.

12 *Pritzker Prize speech*.

13 Like the Italian critic VM Lampugnani, for instance. See his editorials in *Domus* magazine [Nos 734 and 757].

14 Nobel, David F [1997] *The Religion of Technology: the Divinity of man and the Spirit of Invention*.

Lifts/Elevators

Theoretical calculations are an essential element of lift design and these ensure that any structure provides the basic requirements in terms of lift numbers, load and speed. However the performance of the lifts should far exceed the theoretical results.

The technology for this is an integrated package whereby the stored knowledge is continually refined and the lift performance continues to improve. Landing calls assignments for example are constantly reviewed and updated at least twice per second. In addition, once a day the previous day's statistics are saved and exponential smoothing is applied. The result is a substantial database of accurate and specific information about the commercial tower building. Forecasts are made for every day of the week, giving each day an individual profile. As a result, lift

performance improves progressively as the control system learns about its operating environment.

The linear drive motor system is a world first in high rise application with the power to weight ratio, energy consumption and heat losses surpassing all previous designs. The larger sheaves and steel core ropes employed lessen rope bending stress and thereby extend rope life and substantially reduce disruption to tenants.

Lift cabins too are of special design which provides 'whisper-quiet operation' and also allow car interior refits without a future compromise of ride comfort.

The ADM door system also provides smooth swift and silent operation which maximises passenger confidence by eliminating unnecessary contact between doors and users.

All of the above elements combine to ensure that each individual lift is world class. However, it is the artificial intelligence and genetic algorithm which are the key elements in this integration.

Light

Opposite A terracotta balcony wall of a winter garden adjacent to the eastern louvred facade.
Following Pages A close-up of a fritted glass panel showing the vertical 'dogbone' on the right which supports the glass.

I love working with very light elements.
I love transparency, I love natural light.[1]

To construct an interpretive framework for Renzo Piano's architecture it is salutary to consider both light and lightness. For Piano and the Building Workshop, light is as important a theme as any that defines their work. In their architecture light and the aesthetic sense of lightness are deployed to make visible or 'bring forth' social, cultural and tectonic truths; to articulate a particular spatiality; to assemble transparencies and layering; and to de-materialise substantive elements.

We live in an age where certitude of knowledge, wisdom and truth are attained through vision. In the absence of these aptitudes we risk being seen as 'blind' or 'in the dark.' Vision has been the most privileged of the senses since the Renaissance, our certitude comes in an age where for something to be proven it must be seen. We customarily refer to the antecedent epoch as a dark age and a crucial phase of the subsequent period we call the enlightenment. The printed page not only codifies knowledge but asserts a claim to authority as the site of accurate reference and the place to see what is, or what has happened. Since the emergence of the printed book in the second half of the 15th century Western culture has almost stopped listening in the sense that there can be an oral dimension to culture and has become ocular-centric.[2]

In architecture, the very image of modernity is substantially derived from the interaction of light and human vision articulated through the tectonic manipulation of enclosing elements, openings, glazing and interior spaces. The materiality of architecture now largely consists of glass and the other, which is often that which supports the glass. Openness or open planning of interior spaces generously illuminated with natural light and divisions or boundaries between spaces that are not solid but dependent on transparency and light, are sacred parts of modern architecture's historical appeal for superior authority. The architecture of glass and light was an important desideratum of the modernist pioneers in the first half of the last century.

Light

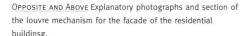

OPPOSITE AND ABOVE Explanatory photographs and section of the louvre mechanism for the facade of the residential buildinsg.

Although the social and cultural implications of such a striving are not talked about now in architectural circles, they were then. Walter Benjamin, the cultural critic who was associated with the Frankfurt School of Social Research in the 1930s is a case in point: 'The twentieth century, with its porosity, transparency, light and free air made an end to living in the old sense.[3]' He appraised the 18th century Parisian arcades as a case of prescient modernism and planned [but never completed] an extended cultural analysis on the theme of modernity and vision that the famous glass roofed arcades invoked for him. Benjamin regretted though that things made of glass seemed to lack what he called 'aura' meaning they were prosaic and insubstantial compared to the subtlety of things wholly or partially concealed. However, he was sympathetic to the progressive vision that he found in Paul Scheerbart's extraordinary 1914 essay 'Glass Architecture'. In this he prophesied an architecture of glass and steel that a century later we find in the work of many contemporary architects, Renzo Piano among them.

If we want our culture to rise to a higher level, we are obliged, for better or for worse, to change our architecture. And this only becomes possible if we take away the closed character of the rooms in which we live. We can only do that by introducing glass architecture, which lets in the light of the sun, the moon, and the stars, not merely through a few windows, but through every possible wall, which will be made entirely of glass—of coloured glass. The new environment which we thus create, must bring us a new culture.[4]

In 'Glass Architecture' Scheerbart, wrote a manifesto about a different architecture. His vision included such things as double glass walls for heating and cooling, glass bricks, lighting between the double walls, light columns and light towers, movable partitions, the end of the window; the loggia and the balcony, ghostly illumination, the crystal room illuminated by translucent floors and airports as glass palaces. Most of these uncanny predictions have now been delivered in the glass architecture of many contemporary architects, Renzo Piano and his Building Workshop among them.

Of course this is not to argue for Piano as the premier glass architect, but to place his work in a progressive mainstream that is now nine decades old. In Piano's case though it is hard to separate light and transparency from light construction and what he calls immateriality—they are congruent and part of his conception of space in architecture. For example, in his *Logbook* he sketches something of the difference:

I have spoken of immaterial elements. These are such things as light, transparency, vibration, texture and colour: elements that interact with the form of the space [in some cases they are a consequence of it] but are not just a function of it. I started out, in an ingenuous, even rather primitive way, from lightness.

Anyone can build using a lot of material... Taking weight away from things, however, teaches you to make the shape of structures do the work, to understand the limits of strength of components and to replace rigidity with flexibility... When you are looking for lightness, you find something else that is precious and that is very important on the plane of poetic language: transparency. By taking things away you also remove the opacity from material.

Lightness is an instrument and transparency is a poetic quality: this is a very important difference.[5]

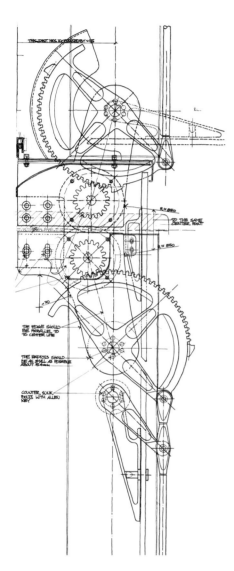

SECTION SHOWING OPERATION OF GLASS LOUVRES

Facades of Commercial Tower

Being oriented towards the rising and setting sun, exposure of the East and West Facades to lower angle solar radiation has led to them being conceived as technically advanced smooth, white protective 'shell-like' skins.

As they project up and out into space they 'dematerialise' the mass of the building and serve as protective screens to the north and south facing wintergardens.

These curving facades are made up of open jointed panelized glazing fixed with structural silicone. The white colour is achieved by the use of a single laminated white fritted pane of low-iron glass throughout the fins, sail, spandrel and column panels. On the large vision panels, the frit fades away to reveal a bright, clear, mildly reflective window to the view.

The geometry of the fritted glass facade and the detailing inside, add a unique quality to the office spaces behind this curtain wall.

The sweeping arcs of the building's geometry are reflected on the internal surface with a gentle curve to the window plane.

The coherent nature of the interior is principally the result of the flush sills and splayed internal reveals, which not only frame the east and west views but also soften the contrast between the vision panels and the mullions.

This softening effect is further enriched by the diminishing frit pattern which extends into the vision panel. These internal elements are smooth and rounded in direct contrast to the detailing on the north and south facades.

The architectural design criteria for these facades lie in the way they contrast with those on the east and west. This idea of contrast is manifested in their appearance as shaded recesses within the shelter of the luminescent white fins.

High solar angles in combination with protective east and west fins allow full

height, floor-to-ceiling vision glass to the north and south. Direct solar impact is minimised by the use of horizontal louvre sunshades. This facade treatment maximises the views to the Opera House and Harbour.

In contrast to the glazing on the east and west, the north and south facades are not smooth and flush, but use expressed mullions and a large horizontal tubular 'bracket' which clearly marks the floor levels. Across the north facade, this bracket accepts the 'leaf-spring' strut, the horizontal aluminium catwalk and sunshade system, and the exterior lighting.

Where semi-enclosed wintergardens are located on the north and south elevations, electrically driven louvres provide direct contact with the external environment on each floor.

These are exciting spaces that mediate between the interior and exterior of the commercial tower and maximise the experience of Sydney's temperate climate.

Glass

The glazing of Aurora Place was intended to achieve an almost ghostly white mysterious presence. Initial prototypes using clear glass with a white ceramic frit applied to one face quickly proved that clear glass would not produce the desired effect. The problem was that the iron content in the sands used to produce what might loosely be described as 'normal' glass caused a mild green tint. When the ceramic frit was applied, this resulted in a facade that had a greenish-white appearance.

Further prototypes were made, this time using low-iron glass which is virtually crystal clear. However hitherto this type of glass had only been used to make retail display units where high clarity was necessary and not to dress a 44 storey tower with a surface area the equivalent of 20 soccer pitches.

Further investigations revealed that there were only three suppliers in the world who made low-iron glass. Moreover, it was only produced once a year due to the specially controlled environment required. Three full-scale prototypes were then made, two of which were mobile so that they could be viewed from various aspects and orientations before approval by the developers and RPBW.

Piano is disturbed by what he calls the ancestral association of house with shelter, protection and solidity—the '...circumscribed concept of space.' He argues for a different conception, proposing what he calls 'a less suffocating idea of architectural space'. Importantly he categorises his own '...space of architecture' as '...a microcosm, an inner landscape.'[6] He instances the idea of inner landscape with a reference to Brancusi's original Paris studio which the sculptor viewed as a metaphorical Romanian forest. Is there then a case for arguing that Piano's architecture attempts a recovery of the territory of the 'aura' that Benjamin lamented losing in modernism? There is some evidence for this being so at Aurora Place, particularly in the façades of the office tower. Here the finishing cantilever of the façade over the vertical and horizontal enclosing perimeter of the building, fabricates a 'sail' metaphor in response to Sydney's harbour, but the glass also undergoes a "...transition to nothing" through the intensity of the dot screen frit coating reducing towards the edges. The same visual fading or dematerialising treatment occurs in other projects, for example in the enveloping wood screens at the Tjibaou Cultural Centre in New Caledonia. Piano, writing in his *Logbook* says there is a '...logical and poetical continuity' about 'working with light in the quest for lightness and transparency. Natural light [often diffused from above] is a constant feature of my work.' In another reference to the poetic, diffused quality that attends much of the Workshop's exercises in working with light, lightness and immateriality he continued: 'To exploit the quality of light we have often created spaces with multiple and successive vertical planes.' He illustrates this with reference to the sense of infinity that a layering of this type creates at the Menil Museum in Houston, and then concludes with yet another auratic reference:

Light is not just an intensity, but also a vibration, which is capable of roughening a smooth material, of giving a three-dimensional quality to a flat surface. Light, colour, and texture are part of a patient work in progress in my studio.[7]

In his 1998 Pritzker Prize citation address, Piano extended this and returned again to the misunderstanding about his idea of tranparency:

My insistence on transparency is often misunderstood and interpreted as insensitivity to the 'space' of architecture. Of course space is made up of volumes; high and low volumes, compressions and expansions, calm and tension, horizontal planes and inclined planes. They are all elements intended to stir the emotions, but they are not the only ones. I believe that it is a very important to work with the immaterial elements of space. I think this is one of the main currents in my architecture.

At Aurora Place the transparency theme is arguably the main theme. In a 2000 television documentary[8] Piano began his retelling of the project's design thinking by declaring that office towers normally don't tell '...a nice story' and then recounted the Workshop's decision to '...create a series of outdoor spaces, to create social points and to increase transparency.' After considering the office tower as a building type, Piano felt that it was time to '...construct a transparent tower.' In this imagined sequence of future events, as well as pushing for the wintergardens on each office floor as communal, breakout spaces, the architect's social agenda for the tower building included transparency, as a means of seeing people inside the office space. Thus in office work there is no privacy; Scheerbart's call for us to abandon the intimacy of rooms has been met. In fact, it had been met by the end of the 1920s when Benjamin wrote 'everything to come stands under the banner of transparency.'[9] And by the end of the 1950s the transparent glass wall, used by pioneer modernists to unite interior and exterior and to create a sense of social parity between the occupants of both realms, became the '...very index of capitalist corporate exclusivity.'[10] As an index of the separation of office life from private life, it is interesting to note that transparency hasn't permeated domestic architecture in anything like the same degree. Discussing an isolated example of transparency in domestic life in Mies van der Rohe's Farnsworth House, sociologist Richard Sennett noted that:

...all the normal signs of domesticity become obscure. Instead this is a space in which we experience the terror of nature sharpened by a building offering no promise of refuge. It is a modern expression of the sublime.[11]

At Aurora Place however, the offices are not transparent in the sense that they are fully sheathed in clear glass. Instead the glass fritting design is arranged to create a regular pattern of clear glass 'windows' in the otherwise smooth glass façade. From inside and out, this looks like a window pattern of more traditional orientation, even though the whole assemblage is made from the one material—glass. For the residents of the apartments at Aurora Place though, glass and transparency present no such terror. The side facing the office tower has a glass treatment identical to that of its neighbour and that facing Macquarie Street has a 'thermal cushion' glass wall over the face of balconies which form and grade the sense of privacy on the inside of the apartments. With all its permutations and combinations, this layered approach to light, lightness, immateriality, transparency and interiority is sufficiently flexible to do many things simultaneously. The interior/exterior boundary

or edge is an important juncture in the Building Workshop's architectural system where light is filtered and manipulated, vision is controlled and selectively permitted free reign, space is arranged and shaped by light and intimacy is permitted. Light is the common element and vision is instrumental in the bringing forth.

1 Renzo Piano interviewed on *The Newshour With Jim Lehrer,* 19June, 1998.

2 Levin, David Michael, Ed. [1993] *Modernity and the Hegemony of Vision.*

3 Quoted in Buck-Morss, Susan [1991] *The Dialectics of Seeing; Walter Benjamin and the Arcades Project.*

4 Sharp, D, ed. [1972] *GlassArchitecture* by *Paul Scheerbart and Alpine Architecture by Bruno Taut.*

5 Piano, R [1997] *Renzo Piano Logbook,* p 253

6 *Logbook* p253.

7 *Logbook,* p253.

8 *Piece by Piece,* screened Australian Broadcasting Commission, 3/9/00.

9 Quoted in Missac, P[1995] *Walter Benjamin's Passages,* p158.

10 Burgin, V [1996] *In Different Spaces; Place and Memory in Visual Culture.*

11 Sennett, R [1990] *The Conscience of the Eye; The design and Social Life of Cities,* p113.

Product

OPPOSITE The terracotta wall of a breakfast nook in the residential building catches the rainbow effect caused by sunlight hitting the bevelled edge of the glass louvres.

Renzo Piano has described his architectural process as 'piece by piece', which is not to say piecemeal, but an assemblage of varied elements, parts and components that arise from the exigencies of the project's architectural program and general design objectives. The pieces are also derived from consideration of context [the place of the project and all its ramifications], climate, available building technologies, ecological imperatives and construction—the act of assemblage.

In his brief forward to the Renzo Piano *Logbook* [1997] Kenneth Frampton cryptically focuses attention on what he calls '...the topographic character of the site and the mode of production'[1] in Piano's architecture. He calls these the presence of ' ...an implicit opposition between Placeform and Produktform' which is resolved at the Menil Museum in Houston. This and the next chapter deal with these two characteristics.

The list of architectural 'products' which are brought forth at Aurora Place begins with the office tower glass facades with their 'fins' and 'sails'. It then goes on to include the thermal cushion glass façade of the apartment building, the office tower wintergardens, the terracotta cladding used on both buildings. Finally there is the glass canopy suspended between the two buildings. It is difficult to draw a line at that point and say that's a list of the products, because all parts of these buildings are carefully designed to the exacting standards, not of architecture, but of industrial design. Aurora Place contains a raft of design products, but these are the main ones. In Heideggerian terms these pieces of products 'exhibit' the world of production and thus share status with the art object.[2] This is something Renzo Piano would probably resist.

At Aurora Place each piece, or product confirms the values of craft design production. In that they communicate what they are and how we should use them, they are readable.[3] The apartment building's operable glass louvres for instance, have all of their mechanical parts exposed to view. *(continued on page 110)*

BELOW AND RIGHT Typical floor to floor view through the east louvre facade of the residential building showing the versatility of the louvres and detailing of the glass and terracotta.

Commercial Lobby

The main aim of the design was to create a simple, uncomplicated, yet dignified lobby and to help ensure its relevance well beyond the passage of changing architectural fashions, a limited palette of materials was used.

On a level platform, the lobby is an extension of the piazza with minimal distinction between inside and out. The green exfoliated granite paving was selected because of its local context. This same granite in the piazza provides an impressive and logical extension into the office building lobby.

The high degree of transparency through the ground floor makes the activity and artwork in the lobby part of the adjacent streets. Simple low-iron glazing is supported by tall elegant steel mullions with sculptured cast ends. This delicate touch is further exploited with the flush detail along the glass line at floor and ceiling and serves to minimise visual separation between the lobby and both the piazza and Phillip Street. The tall, floor-to-ceiling glass allows the daylight to penetrate well into the lobby.

As a calm continuation of the glass canopy over the piazza, the lobby ceiling is strongly up-lit, more intensely at the edges to reduce the contrast with the outside.

The interior lobby space lends itself to a series of lounge areas with direct access to cafe facilities in the piazza. Simple yet elegantly detailed terracotta tiled walls imply warmth and provide a substantial backdrop to a series of carefully placed large-scale public artworks.

The terracotta walls and granite floors contrast with the softer more intimate timber finishes in the concierge and lift lobbies. Here a kind of 'world of wood' is found. It has wide Tasmanian Oak boards with minimal joints on the floor and walls, while the ceiling is lined with timber veneered panels. These panels serve an acoustic role and combined with the warmer recessed down lights create a quieter intimate ambience, heightening the contrast with the busy larger lobby space and piazza outside.

Product

Even though they are automatically operated, one can see all the rods, pins, levers and cogs that engage and move the pivoting glass blades. In the office tower wintergardens, the mechanisms that create the flow of natural ventilation though louvres are similarly presented. Providing readability in material objects like this is part of the social responsibility of designing that should occur at all levels—from door handles to buildings to cities. Offering utility in this way is actually an assertion of belief in the value of the maker/user relationship that should be fundamental to all design but isn't always where function is subordinated to aesthetics.

In Piano's products, aesthetic value is established out of the process of designing, fabricating and assembling objects or elements which embody technological rationality and utility as well as a belief in the value of a direct presentation of a product's constituent materials. Like other Building Workshop products, the terracotta cladding which is used extensively at the street level of Aurora Place and selectively on the upper floors, manifests forms and textures which bear the direct imprint of its manufacturing, fabricating and assembling process. Terracotta is an additive natural substance as distinct from a subtractive natural material like wood or stone that is milled or dressed down. Terracotta attains its final form through the stages of being in a dry state, a wet plastic state, being moulded, then fired and finally assembled and fixed into its final position on the building. The Building Workshop's comprehensive approach is not merely to use a finished product but to form a design intersection at all six stages in the process, thus ensuring a maximum level of control over both the means of production and assembly.

The design outcome of this is that the Produktform reflects the stages of production in a precision that would be expected of an industrial designer who draws, computes, models, prototypes, recycles and prototypes again and again before manufacturing. In contrast other architects might specify 'products' to be delivered to site and fixed in place without any involvement in the production process at all.

The RPBW products are in continual development through a number of iterations on a number of building projects experimenting and testing variations to basic models at each application. The terracotta product at Aurora Place, for example, has antecedents going back [arguably] to the Menil Museum [1982–86] where Piano used manufactured units [timber planks] in a repetitive modular fashion fitted into a steel frame. For the reasons of selecting a panelling system in response to an historical context, terracotta was used at the IRCAM extension in Paris [1988–90] in steel frames just after it was first used in combination with GRC framing and panelling at the Rue de Meaux Housing, also in Paris [1987–91]. At the Cité Internationale de Lyon [1991–95] the terracotta cladding system is used extensively as is the suspended glass canopy and the glass 'thermal cushion' wall. After that the Building Workshop used stone facing cut into precise modular units with some perforated with slats to create an effect of transparency at the Credito Bank project in Cagliari [1985–92]. The terracotta system went through further iterations at the Columbus International Exposition in Genoa [1984–92] and at the Banca Popolare di Lodi [1991–98]. At the Potsdamer Platz reconstruction in Berlin [1992–99] it reached the level of refinement that has informed the Sydney project.[4]

Similarly, the glass canopy suspended between buildings or groups of buildings on the same site emerged in proto form at the Cité Internationale, Lyons, reappeared in a much refined form at the Banca Popolare in Lodi and has been further refined at Aurora Place. The 'thermal cushion' idea of a wide ventilated cavity between two sheets of clear glass also emerged at Lyons and was further developed at Potsdamer Platz before appearing again at the Aurora Place apartment building on Macquarie Street, Sydney.

Terracotta, of all the Building Workshop products constitutes a theme through its being used the most often and through it being a truly innovative product, described here [at Rue de Meaux] by Kenneth Frampton:

Here the fabric of the building is greatly enriched through a subtle interplay between different components set within a 90 cm grid. Naturally, where light is required this module is filled with glass, shielded where required with glass-fibre reinforced cement [GRC] louvres. However the most innovative aspect by far is the cladding of the opaque walls. In this instance the 90 x 90 cm coffered GRC panels, cast from steel moulds, are faced with six 20 x 42 cm terracotta tiles that are quite literally hung onto lugs cast integrally with the back of the panel. This incidental Semperian treatment, in which a building is faced with large loose tiles [a literal bekleidung in fact] seems to me to exemplify exactly a realistic but subtle metaphorical approach whereby rationalised modular production comes to be inflected in such a way as to be both popularly accessible and profoundly evocative of tradition[5]

The design precision of terracotta panelling is an accomplishment that was not possible without enormous labour being expended in research, experimentation, modelling and testing, initially by RPBW and then refined by Bovis Lend Lease. Adopting the production standards of contemporary industry in preference to the contemporary construction site, they have made a virtue out of precision and an aesthetic out of production itself.

Design form alone doesn't always seem to be a starting point in the development of new products. It seems significant that the physical context of some key Workshop products has been the trigger for thinking. For example, at Houston's Menil Museum the timber plank cladding was selected as part of a contextual response to the surrounding residential suburb. At the IRCAM extension in Paris the timber was replaced with terracotta as a strategy to build a contextual dialogue with an older brick neighbour. In the design process consideration of any number of design imperatives like these takes place simultaneously. The specificity of the resultant architecture is not arbitrary or obsessively wrung out of a formalist equation, but developed out of a carefully considered set of intersecting criteria.

[1] Piano, R [1997] *Renzo Piano Logbook*, p7.
[2] Vattimo, G [1988] *The End of Modernity*, p61.
[3] Lampugnani, VM 'The Craft of Design' in *Domus* No 734, January 1992.
[4] This material and that on the other products has been taken from Buchanan, P [1993–2000] vols 1-4.
[5] Frampton, K [1995] *Studies in Tectonic Culture* p385.

Terracotta

Terracotta, which has been used in this project as an internal and external cladding material, has a human scale whilst also providing a layered, earthy texture in contrast to the smooth crystalline glazing.

It is used in three main areas in the design of the two buildings: firstly as an opaque cladding with shadow grooves on the façade. Next as a fine batten screen to mask mechanical grilles and for privacy on the residential apartments, and lastly as a smooth, curved cladding to the columns.

These three basic terracotta types have been developed and refined through experience in a range of built projects since 1987. The intention has always been to generate the architectural ideas and expression through an understanding of manufacturing and construction issues.

With a direct reference to the existing streetscapes, the chosen terracotta colour tends towards an orange sandstone-like hue. Minor variations in the colour over the façade is of course desired, rendering an overall natural softness to the building.

Several other Sydney buildings such as the Grace Building, the Hotel Intercontinental and in particular BMA House in Macquarie Street have terracotta cladding systems which add a warmth and crafted quality to their facades. The natural earthy quality of unglazed terracotta used in Aurora Place 'ties' the buildings both to the ground and the surrounding cityscape.

From outside, the terracotta cladding can be seen to extend from the ground floor to the top of the tower lift cores, over 150 metres high. This not only works in terms of a 'city scale', but the

visual hierarchy between the terracotta panels, the aluminium supports and the various joint types creates a sensitive human scale and a delicate yet tangible architectural expression to the project.

Canopy

The ground plane unifies a network of walkways across the site and repeats the pattern of laneways off historic Macquarie Street that link with the smaller Phillip Lane. At pedestrian level the precinct is unified by the austral verde granite paving extending under both buildings to the road edge. The canopy was generated by extending the radial module grids between both buildings to create a 'spider's web' that binds the project together. The two way grid of light tensile cables supports a plane of low-iron glass slightly bellied to shed rainwater. This deflects the down draft from the buildings and shelters the piazza; more symbolically it binds together the curved white fritted glass facades of both buildings.

For the architects, there were several precedents for this project in Europe including the restructuring of the Schlumberger facilities and more recently the new Banca Popolare head office where the suspended glass links the buildings to a new central auditorium. It was this double catenary cable above and below the glass which was the starting point for Aurora Place.

The cable net found its optimum shape once the edge points were defined. A study was undertaken to comprehend the effect of the geometry in shaping the individual node pieces. The edge plates are all positioned on the curtain wall mullion modules 1350mm on the tower side and 1750 mm on the residential side. The height is determined by the shaping requirements for the anticlastic curve.

The stainless steel 'spiders' joining the glass panels are positioned vertically under the node points of the net. Initial shapes considered were falls from the centre through the facade on each side, to an internal perimeter gutter. The decision was taken to separate the building façade from the canopy glass and a 200mm edge gap exists around the perimeter. After further modelling it was decided the canopy should be horizontal at the edge to align with the curtain wall transoms on either side. These constraints then generated the current belly shape draining to a single low point with a cantilevered scoop in Phillip Lane.

The hovering lightweight canopy together with the large sensuous marble sculptures of Kan Yasuda make the piazza at Aurora Place a memorable civic meeting place.

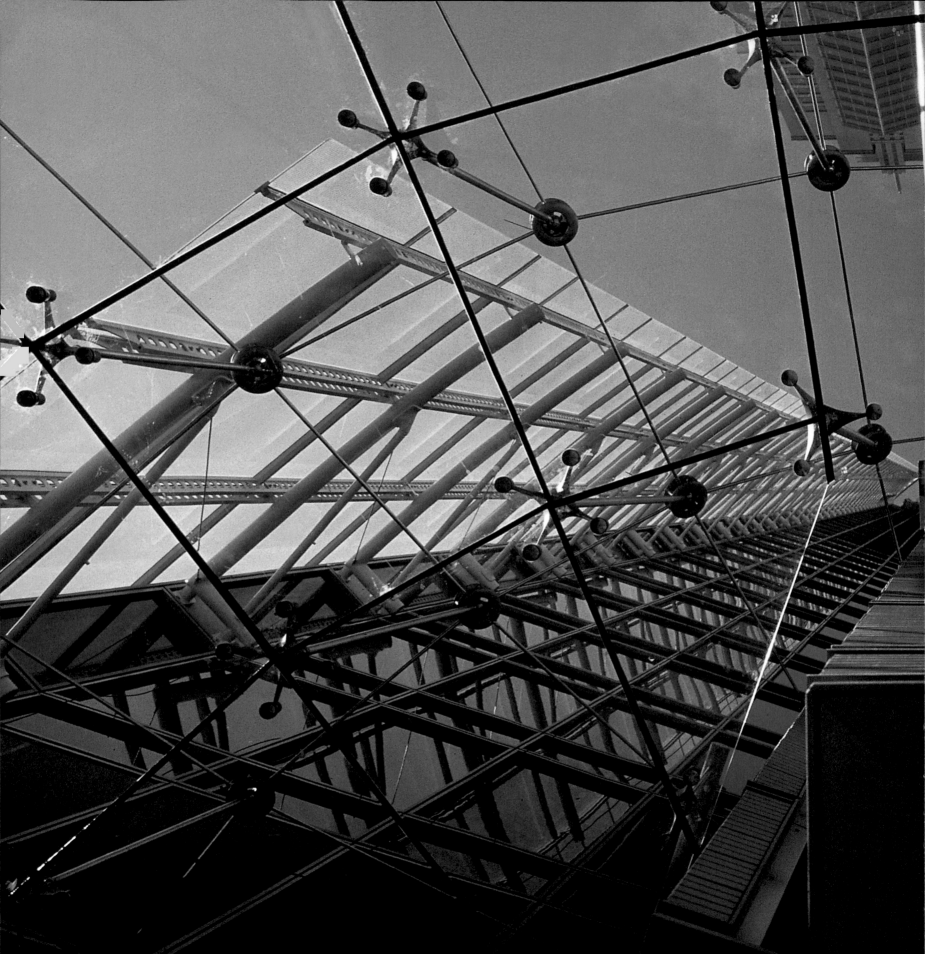

Piazza

Covered by its expansive web-like glass canopy, the piazza between the two towers is destined to become a major meeting place in Sydney both day and night. Cafes spill out from beneath the residential tower with tables and chairs sheltered by the hovering horizontal plane of glass.

The space is bordered by mature plane trees along the southern edge and the large, mysteriously smooth marble 'touchstones' increase the tension between the two curving glass facades of the commercial and the residential buildings as they meet the ground. The marble sculpture is spotlit at night, creating a presence, which is used to illuminate the rest of the piazza.

The aim of the design was to extend an inviting pedestrian precinct through the length of Phillip Lane which, with its shops will give a dense and active European feeling to the piazza.

122

Place

OPPOSITE Level 18 of the residential building showing the relationship of the 450 louvred roof (left) and the wrap-around west sail (right).

FOLLOWING PAGE View to the NE showing the 450 roof of the commercial building and part of the mast.

"...every kind of building has a different story and is in a different place and you cannot consider coherence to make the building equal. I mean coherence is to be able to understand the situation and make a good interpretation."[1]

In Kenneth Frampton's diagrammatic analysis of Renzo Piano's architecture, produktform is in a relationship of tension with placeform.[2] Frampton contends it is this tension which animates much of Piano's architecture. If, as we have seen, produktform entails a precise control of a building's production process; using 'place' implies a detailed and specific knowledge of everything to do with the place of a building. Which is not just the building's actual site but its physical attributes such as the extant architecture neighbouring the site and in the locality, the urban form of the locality and other characteristics such as the site's history, climate and topography.

Maybe in talking about place, Piano studiously avoids using the more common architectural term 'context'

because it has become hackneyed. However, the late 20th century discourse on architecture is heavily inflected by the notion of context, and in architectural historical terms it is likely that what Piano does will be described as 'contextualism'. In this chapter we will defer to Piano's use of the term 'place' but will need to say something on contextualism as well.

Piano has consciously worked with ideas about place, and particularly with the visual metaphors that often animate buildings and their settings, from the time of the Pompidou Centre [1971–78] to the present. For example he describes the 100,000 square metre art museum as impossible to fit in with the houses of the Marais quarter. Nonetheless he calls the building he designed with Richard Rogers a medieval village and a celibate machine. In the end, the Pompidou Centre attempts to form a relationship with its urban setting through its architectural expression and form and also by means of the massive open square the building sits on.[3]

Before tracking the approach to place that piano has adopted in the Aurora Place project it would be salutary to briefly look at contextualism. From around 1970 onwards the field of architectural theory grew away from the limited monotheistic, rhetorical talk of geometry and machine that constituted modernism, to the present polytheistic range of ideas that is commonly known as postmodernism— again a cliched term but still accurate. A large part of the debate has evolved around the relationship that an architecture has—or doesn't have—with previous architectures, specifically, in the case of the city, with neighbouring buildings which can be said to be part of the physical context for architecture.

In a seminal essay[4], that made a crucial contribution to this discussion, the Chicago architect Stuart Cohen, characterised modern architecture as a '...revolution whose ideas succeeded and whose anticipated utopia never ensued...' and dryly noted modern architecture's '...insistence on a cultural, symbolic and physical detachment from aspects of an existing context.' Thus modern architecture appeared to condemn all other architecture by exclusion. Cohen, and before him, Robert Venturi and Denise Scott-Brown[5] pejoratively labelled modern architecture 'exclusivist' and, instead, presented an 'inclusivist' approach that would take full account of a whole raft of material derived from a building's setting such as the style, form, material, texture and colour of existing buildings as well as the site's climate, topography and history.

Piano's own contextual approach has evolved, presumably with knowledge of these developments, towards a form of 'partnership' with the surroundings:

What interests me is shaping form and product together: forcefully sculpting the land, leaving a deep mark on the pre-existing nature or urban structure; but, at the same time, making architecture an accomplice, a partner with the characteristics of the surroundings.

Piano's procedure at Aurora Place has been discriminately to examine the context for effective cues that might be included metaphorically in architectural form. For Piano the primary challenge of the Sydney project has been to create such a relationship, or 'partnership' with Jorn Utzon's Opera House and he seized on this straight away:

The nearest reference, and one that cannot be ignored, is Jorn Utzon's Sydney Opera House, which is one of the city's symbols. Above all it is only a kilometre away. A dialogue between the two objects will be inevitable.[6]

Apart from the building's fame the probable reasons for this are that, for an outsider the Opera House is the city's symbol, for architects it is still a cause celebre about design integrity and an influential icon. The Opera House is also associated with Peter Rice the structural engineer from the multinational Arups firm who worked with Piano on all his projects until his death in 1992. Piano's readiness to start a dialogue may also indicate his own need to pay homage to Utzon as one architect to another.

At Aurora Place the gesture to the Opera House is evident in the billowing sail-like façades and especially in the scalloped crown of the office tower which soars above the building's bulk. Thus, in Piano's discriminating gaze, the Opera House is privileged over other architecture much closer to hand including two significant office towers and a cluster of smaller buildings right down to terrace houses on Macquarie and Phillip Streets. So, for Piano, place is a selective process, not an inclusive one; this distinguishes his practice from the American led contextualist orthodoxy of the 1970s and 1980s. Never distracted by fashion or opinion, Piano has appropriated and re-invented the contextualist procedure, that significant numbers of contemporary critics now ignore, or worse, deride as outdated.

There are other aspects of place that have been mulled over by Piano and the Building Workshop. Firstly, there is the component of the site's history. For Piano this is taken to mean extant buildings nearby, especially those on Macquarie Street which have the predominantly masonry presentation typical of the terracotta material used in the lower reaches of both the buildings at Aurora Place. Here again the procedure is selective and doesn't include any detailed reference to the site's actual history as we have seen. Also to the point is the way the gesture to traditional masonry has been used to strengthen the Building Workshop's use of the terracotta theme familiar from other projects. Secondly, at Aurora Place Piano has responded to Sydney, '...a young city' he calls it, by making his project contribute emphatically to what he calls a '...solidification and settling"[7] of the urban fabric. He has done this by constructing a building complex that is both a landmark and likely to have some permanence [particularly the apartment building which is strata-titled], and is forcefully 'grounded' by use of the terracotta material that is compatible with the locality itself. Thirdly there is a social dimension to the creation of place. Sensitive to the risk of creating another dumb office building like a 'tower of Babel', the Renzo Piano Building Workshop have proposed, fought for and delivered the

'social spaces' [wintergardens] on each office floor which effectively become points of socialisation placed at the interval of each floor. But the 'social space' concept does not end there. The covered piazza at street level which required the part closure and re-routing of Phillip Lane can be seen as an extension of the existing network of plazas, places and piazzas that humanise the CBD.

And, finally, climate is a signature part of the Building Workshop's agenda for responding to place. Like the sails and crown in a dialogic relationship with the Opera House, the architects' insistence on natural cross-ventilation to augment air conditioning through the use of banks of operable glass louvres, adds a site-specific dimension to the architecture. Surely it is appropriate that the inhabitants not just view the world outside but actually experience it. The varying fenestration patterns that occupants make on the apartment building façade are what Piano referred to as a living, breathing piece of sculpture, description seized upon by the developers with their sales slogan: 'art you can live in.'

The interactive tension between place and product at Aurora Place, and indeed, in other Piano projects underpins the experience of architecture. It is an experience that one gets in contact with objects that are derived from the recognisable and the ordinary as distinct from the abstract and the arcane. Architectural configurations like the glass louvres and the terracotta panelling at Aurora Place are firmly connected with the familiar and the recognisable. Appreciating them and seeing their use in more sophisticated settings like this invoke a subconscious thought that these things are part of a shared material culture that is everybody's common property. The use of familiar items on the conscious interplay

between architecture and locality at Aurora Place builds a tangible architectural spatiality that contrasts sharply with the ubiquitous sense of simultaneity of virtual reality of cyber space. So too do the other contemporary non-places of mass society that are unrelated to physical boundaries or not specific to any one site. Over time this capacity of architecture to construct site specificity will probably become more important: architecture that speaks about a place to the people of a place is a very old conception but a necessary one.

1 Renzo Piano interviewed on 'The News Hour with Jim Lehrer', 19/6/98.
2 Renzo Piano [1997] *Renzo Piano Logbook*, Frampton's preface, p7.
3 *Logbook*, p40.
4 Cohen, S 'Physical Context/Cultural Context: Including it All', *Oppositions 2*, January 1974.
5 Venturi, R and Scott-Brown, D [1984] *A View from the Campidoglio; Selected Essays 1953–1984*.
6 *Logbook*, p242.
7 *Logbook*, p242.

Exterior Lighting

The basic design intent for the façade lighting was simply to reinforce the key architectural ideas for the project; to create a gentle ghostly white presence, which is in 'dialogue' with the Sydney Opera House. The new building's curving glass presence is stitched into the local context with a spine of terracotta which transforms into an orthogonal 'cityscape'. The north and south glass facades remain as dark recesses.

The exterior lighting was not designed just for special events, but suited for use throughout the year. For efficient and effective maintenance, bulbs will be changed in one operation once every five years, not one at a time. The whole lighting system was set up to be controlled by building management, not tenants. It was designed to 'clothe' the building at night from 9 or 10 pm when the offices were empty and after cleaners had gone and internal lights had been switched off and blinds drawn. The most important visual feature of

this project is the architectural integrity and gentleness of the east and west curving facades. By night these facades are washed with warm up-lights which fade towards the top but then pick out the edges and fins. This is achieved using 'spidery' outreach arms projecting out of the base of the glass area on both east and west facades.

The extremities of the fins read like 'sketched lines' in the night — vertical edges only, not the sail profiles. It is important to note that Renzo Piano expected that his 'sketch' idea would be evaluated both visually and technically. It should also be noted that the fish scale of the south-east corner is strongly expressed by night up-lighting which is desirable.

The terracotta cladding systems adds warmth, human scale and crafted quality to the project. By night the aim was to enhance the presence of terracotta by directing a narrow beam of light up the core. In the case of the south spine, the mast is also washed all round.

For the night-time experience of the building in the skyline, the lighting enhances the four principal fins from points as far out from the building as possible.

To experience the building by night at street level the objective was to reinforce the compression between the curving facades and create a welcoming ground plane and laneway.

At the ground plane, the intention was to wash up the east and west curving facades of the office building from outreach arms. The upper part of the residential façade glows from reflected light.

The 'touchstones' sculpture in the piazza is well lit from three directions to create soft shadows with warm light to compensate for the icy quality of the stone. In this way the 'stones' themselves have become a light source.

BMU

The centralised maintenance system relies on one large crane type Building Maintenance Unit (BMU) located at the main roof level. This is capable of reaching all areas on the facade including both sides of the main sail as well as both sides of all projecting fins.

Weighing in the vicinity of 30 tonnes and operating from a fixed position, the unit sits on a heavy duty track which is located on structural steel supports just below the line of the sloping roof.

The BMU has a telescopic jib which can be extended to 55 metres with a luffing capacity enabling it to luff upward to reach over the main sail. It can also luff below horizontal so as to maintain the minimum 15m unrestrained cable length from the tip of the jib to the first restraint point on the east facade.

The method of restraint for the BMU is via lanyards, so that on the outer face, sheaves on each lanyard allow a cable to pass through cleanly. On the inner face, a system comprising a nylon rope on separate spool, allows the cradle to be kept against the facade whilst the main support cables are free to move.

By using a 3D computer model of the building's design, the BMU can access all points on the facade below the main roof levels except for the two steps in the north elevation at approximately levels 12 and three. These are served by monorail mounted swing stages.

This is one of the largest units ever made and has to cope with extraordinary challenges such as a sloping roof and an inclined facade.

Expression

OPPOSITE Position, position, position. Aurora Place seen through the sails of the Sydney Opera House.

The architect can never abandon his specific role of providing the forms.[1]

When Renzo Piano says that a little bit of expression is a good thing but too much is bad, he draws our attention to the issue of communicating through form in architecture, and with it, ideas concerning monuments, ornamentation and decoration. For roughly three quarters of the twentieth century the issue of architectural expression wouldn't have been on the agenda for discussion: the modernist canon accommodated neither ornament nor decoration, although it did tolerate monuments. Ironically much modern movement architecture was monumental in spite of the social covenant of not constructing monuments being widely affirmed [in theory if not in practice].

Perhaps reflecting on these themes in a candid moment and perhaps aware of a particular latent technological formalism in the Building Workshops' architecture, Renzo Piano conceded:

In my architecture, the way something is built is important. That explains why it often slips into decoration and a taste for hi-tech, the pure delight of exhibiting...[2]

Accepting such formalism is just as 'ingenuous and academic' as 19th century historicist styling, Piano allows that making the decorative slip is an ever-present risk and:

One which I don't always manage to avoid because the practice of design, its language and mode of expression are impervious. So a few slip-ups occur. But I want to make it clear that I now understand the point at which building in a certain way turns into gratuitous exhibitionism.[3]

However, one of the numerous creditable accomplishments of Piano's work at Aurora Place is precisely the expressive character of the architecture. When this is tectonically derived, but fully integrated within the 'products' that are built, we readily acknowledge such technologically formalistic elements as achievements; indeed, we expect them from the Building Workshop.

However, in the office tower and to a lesser extent in the apartment building, there exists a level of expression that is unusual for the Piano office, and probably, for this building type—in Australia anyway. It is probable that this is the key departure from orthodoxy to be found at Aurora Place.

It is normal, as Vittorio Gregotti puts it[4] for commercial architecture to exist as a '…mere instrument of mercantile production', and although Piano's Sydney work conforms to this commercial typology, what is new at Aurora Place is that the '…institutional frame'[5] of the commercial office tower itself has been expanded and pushed beyond the norm. A comparison with other building types will show this. For example, the contemporary art gallery or museum is the institutional frame for art, within which a wide variety of architectural expressions is evidently possible. Comparing Piano's several contributions to this field with those of, say, Frank Gehry quickly makes this point. But, if the office tower is the institutional frame of reference for commerce, [which it is] then it is a building type where, hitherto, architectural expression has been tightly reined in. The orthodoxy of the commercial office tower is a cynical response to financial, planning and constructional formulas that usually produces the sort of uninspired, transitory accompaniments to mass society that we have come to expect office buildings to be. Remarkably, the attitude and collaboration of the client enabled a less-inhibited and more sculptural approach at Aurora Place which nevertheless set new benchmarks in commercial leasing.

The metaphorical allusions to Jorn Utzon's Sydney Opera House and to the sails of the harbour are the means through which this expansion of the institutional frame has been accomplished, the vehicle for a freer architectural expression. When Piano promised: 'The ambition is clearly to produce something more memorable than one of Sydney's many skyscrapers'[6] and proceeded to design the buildings façades as 'sails' and reflect the Opera House in the buildings crowns, we can assume he knew of the omnipotence of kitsch. And he must also have known of the critical distinction between that which is necessary for a building to function and that which is surplus. Again the relativity of the Gehry comparison is illuminating—in his case making such a distinction would be pointless.

However the necessity/surplus relationship is a complex one and the context in which it is applied must be analysed. The Renzo Piano Building Workshop has arrived at the sails and crown configuration in the Sydney project through an internally consistent design process that, working at both the general and the particular, has accounted for architecture through the themes of place, light, product, tectonics, materials and, of course, purpose. So, does one specific instance of signification, like the expressive Opera House metaphor, somehow transgress a boundary into decoration, or does one idiomatic lapse amount to a lapse of judgement?

At Aurora Place there is evidence to suggest that this is not the case. Firstly, there is Hans Gadamer's espousal of a broader role for decoration that sees it working initially to attract attention to itself and then redirect it towards the larger context of life in which it is situated.[7] In this context, architecture is, by nature, decorative and Piano's Sydney work is a case in point: there are many layers of detail that work in this manner. Secondly,

Piano sees himself moving not towards decoration, but towards ornament.

In the baroque era, in the 19th century and much of the 20th, ornament was handled in an extraordinarily expressive manner. I believe that architecture has to be given back its richness. In Japanese architecture ...there is a ritual way of building houses with a precise hierarchy of details: from the tatami to the partition... Quality is based on the perfect harmony amongst all of the components... RPBW has taken another look at terracotta, wood and stone... and has tried in some way to 'reinvent' their use.

In spite of the topical nature of the gestures to the Opera House, in Piano's architecture at Aurora Place one does encounter a specific cohesion of structure and ornament. It occurs at the very points where his 'products' like the suspended glass canopy and the terracotta elements and the 'thermal cushion' wall are supported structurally in such a way that structure and ornament are seen to be part of the same idea, the same thinking pattern. Gervok Hartoonian believes that it is at this point that architecture literally becomes ornament.[8]

In the formative period of modernism when the movement went global between say 1925 and 1965, geometry, flat surface and texture were the primary aesthetic means adopted to try and breech the gaping void left by the collapse of classicism. At this time the sort of tectonic attainment that Piano has comprehensively reached in his corpus of work, was rarely known or seen outside the works of Pierre Chareau at his Maison de Verrre in Paris and in the works of the Italian masters, Carlo Scarpa and Franco Albini—the latter a mentor of Piano's. Since 1970, however, tectonic expression has emerged as a sustaining presence in architecture that

might one day develop the power of 'language' once enjoyed by classicism. No doubt the Centre Georges Pompidou in Paris was a breakthrough in this development and, not just Piano but his partner Richard Rogers and his partner's partner Norman Foster, amongst others, have accepted geometry in modernist architecture and made a virtue out of the way something is built.

Arguably, with his sails and crown interpretation of Sydney's 'story' at Aurora Place, Piano goes further towards formalistic expressionism than he has done before. In the office tower the Pianoesque fusion of structure and ornament also becomes an edge that is pushed hard, a boundary that is stretched. These two things alone make the project singular and perhaps one that anticipates a new route.

1 Renzo Piano interviewed by VM Lampugnani, *Domus* No 688, p19.
2 *Domus* No 688, p20.
3 *Domus* No 688, p20.
4 Gregotti, G [1996] p60.
5 Vattimo, G [1988] *The End of Modernity*, p53.
6 Piano, R [1997] *Renzo Piano Logbook* p242
7 Gadamer in 'Truth and Method' cited in Vattimo, p83.
8 Hartoonian, G [1994] *Ontology of Construction*, p88.

Art

OPPOSITE At night Kan Yasuda's while marble 'Touchstones' play with light in the piazza of Aurora Place.

Aurora Place is an enlightened built environment further invigorated by artistic vision, and as a result, home for an important collection of art reflecting both the Australian spirit embodied in this development and its international status. Whilst Lend Lease oversaw the commissioning of each artist, the collection was developed with input from the architect, Renzo Piano[1]. The seven artists chosen to be represented are John Firth-Smith, Bill Henson, Dale Frank, George Rickey, Caio Fonseca, Tim Prentice and Kan Yasuda. Reported to be one of Australia's most valuable corporate art commissions, these works are viewed as considerable contributions to public art.

The three Australian artists, John Firth-Smith, Bill Henson and Dale Frank, whose works were selected for the residential complex are of a quality and calibre that complement the architecture. Each is a significant contemporary artist renowned for his singularity of approach to art and a major contributor to the culture of this country. The artists also represent an excellent investment and are highly sought after for both public and private collections.

For the residential foyer, a John Firth-Smith was chosen, as his large-scale paintings are ideal for big areas. His brilliant use of colour and bold compositions more than hold their own in big architectural spaces, and he is highly experienced in producing work for major buildings. Firth-Smith has exhibited widely in Australia and overseas since the 1960s, and is one of Australia's pre-eminent abstract painters. His work is represented in every major public gallery in Australia, and in 1999 a major monograph was published on his work.

OPPOSITE The installation sequence of placing 'The Touchstones' in the piazza. The sculptor Kan Yasuda is seen in the foreground of the main picture.

Bill Henson's 1985/86 series of urban and suburban peripheries, of a darkening, millennial world with beautiful images of railway underpasses, power lines, city lights, and feral children effectively bring the outdoors indoors and is large and diverse enough to provide a consistent yet varied selection of works for the 30 lobbies of the residential complex. This is an important body of work in his career, and the purchase of a considerable number of these images is a significant investment. Henson is arguably Australia's most acclaimed contemporary photographer. Over his long career, which began in 1975 with a solo show at the National Gallery of Victoria at the age of 20, Henson has represented Australia at the 1995 Venice Biennale and has had numerous exhibitions both in Australia and overseas.

Dale Frank's irreverent yet committed approach to his art, and the vibrant quality of his paintings, made his work an ideal choice for the gym area. Frank has also exhibited extensively in Europe, Australia and the US, including the 1984 Venice Biennale and the 1979, 1982 and 1990 Sydney Biennales. His large, sensual paintings utilise unusual materials such as varnish, tarpaulin and aluminium, creating beauty from the most unexpected sources. Frank is a prolific, diverse yet consistent artist, and a retrospective of his painting was shown in early 2000 at the Museum of Contemporary Art, Sydney.

In total 33 pieces by Australian artists are on display in the residential complex, whilst three international artists were commissioned to create works for the commercial tower lobby.

On the lobby's west side, a kinetic sculpture by American artist George Rickey is suspended from the ceiling. Painter, sculptor and historian, George Rickey was born in Indiana in 1907 and has led a remarkably varied life. A student of the Academie Andre L'hote and Academie Moderne in Paris, he painted from 1930 until his late forties, when he turned to making moveable structures or mobiles, first from glass and then metals. Now, with over four decades of dedicated experimentation, Rickey has forged a vast body of work, bringing him international acclaim as one of the world's foremost kinetic sculptors.

His exquisitely engineered steel sculptures respond to wind and the pull of gravity. Stainless steel shapes are activated and balanced through a system of meticulously engineered counterweights and bearings which are set in motion by air currents. Rickey is less interested in the forms of his sculptures, focusing more on the pattern of their movements. Motion both fascinates and compels Rickey, and the movements of his sculptures are slow, smooth and unpredictable, evoking a mesmerising quality of repetition and variation that captivates the viewer, like ocean waves.

Whether large outdoor sculptures or small intimate table pieces, these silent moving objects continually capture and redefine space.

His work is represented in over 200 public collections world-wide and George Rickey currently lives and works in New York.

Opposite Caio Fonseca's work 'Fifth Street#14'. Below top left
Kan Yasuda's Touchstones cast perfect shadows in the Piazza.
Below bottom left Tim Prentice's installation 'Three Wheeler'
provides action by the coffee shop. Below The exquisitely
engineered kinetic sculpture by George Rickey.

140

Close to the Rickey sculpture hangs a large canvas by Caio Fonseca an American artist who was born in New York in 1959 and who has travelled and studied art in Spain, Uruguay, Italy and Paris. After 14 years abroad, he returned to the USA in 1992 where he set up a studio in downtown New York. Today he divides his time between his studios in Manhattan and Pietrasanta, Italy. His works are held in numerous public and private collections in Europe and the United States.

Fonseca is inspired by a love of music. His canvas will often appear as a lyrical play of tone, rhythm and balance, all elegantly woven with the cadence of a visual counterpoint. The purely abstract works are arranged in quirky compositions which seem, at first encounter, to be random. However, with contemplation, each movement in a Fonseca painting often reveals deft precision. The placement of his signature geometric forms are not bound by gravity to the foregrounds.

His work clearly shows the influences of his modernist forefathers such as Miro and Mondrian, and through his art, Fonseca demonstrates both respect and defiance towards the traditions that are integral parts of his training. However, he has cultivated knowledge of these components, which allows him to escape from his aesthetic heritage.

The lobby east is dominated by a series of circular 'wheels'; a wall installation by Tim Prentice. Originally a gifted and respected architect, Tim Prentice received an MA degree in architecture from Yale University in 1965. On completion of his degree he founded the award winning architectural company Prentice and Chan.

Ten years later, in order to dedicate his time to design and fabricate his large-scale kinetic sculptures, Prentice established a studio in Cornwall, Connecticut where he now lives and works.

As a kinetic sculptor, Prentice works in a variety of lightweight materials including aluminium, stainless steel, feathers and Lexan. His work investigates the shape, form and flow of wind currents in order to make air visible. Prentice's use of intriguing structures and reflective metals enable his sculptures to soar, or undulate, in response to their environment. Architectural training has helped Prentice design commissions with a sensitivity to their surroundings whether they be for large corporations or private collections.

He has held countless solo and group exhibitions, completed installations in Europe, Hong Kong and Japan and has an impressive list of corporate clients. Integral to the design of Aurora Place is the piazza. This is the public, open area that links the two separate buildings and provides protection from the elements by the exquisitely crafted glass canopy. The piazza is both a pedestrian thoroughfare and a social destination with the ambience of an active open-air public meeting place. At its heart are two magnificent marble 'stones', hand sculptured by Japanese artist, Kan Yasuda.

Yasuda's work, titled 'Touchstones' is a splendid example of the marriage of art and architecture. Artists are rarely brought in at the beginning of a project and rarely work directly with architects but Aurora Place was an exception to the rule and the connection between architect and artist was actively encouraged right from the commencement of the project.

Renzo Piano, long impressed by the work of Kan Yasuda, began a dialogue with the internationally acclaimed sculptor in 1997. From there the concept of 'Touchstones' was born. Yasuda shares Renzo's fascination with the contrast between lightness and solidity.

Prior to visiting the site, Yasuda's vision was of two different sized stone sculptures reflecting the harmony and distinction between the tower and the residential building at Aurora Place. But once he stood in the piazza area, during his first visit to Australia in August 1998, Kan Yasuda was moved by a sense of compression between the curving residential and commercial facades and the soaring strength of the tower.

Following his visit to Australia, Yasuda returned to his studio at Pietrasanta in northern Italy, with a new appreciation of the environment in and around Aurora Place. He had combed the Harbour, fascinated by the formation of Sydney Heads and impressed by its stone cliffs. He'd flown over the site to comprehend fully Renzo's notion of a dialogue between Aurora Place and the Opera House.

As a result, 'Touchstones' evolved into two equally sized monolithic 'stones'; individual but inextricably connected—in dialogue, but silent in their solidity. Carved from the magnificent white marble of Carrara, the very same quarries used by Michelangelo, the 'Touchstones' play with light and luminosity; a feature reflecting Renzo's own play on light, so integral to the design of Aurora Place. Two years in the making, 'Touchstones' were hand shaped by Kan Yasuda. Weighing 18 tonnes each, the 'stones' are 2.3 metres high, a little over 3 metres long and 1.5 metres wide. Working with him in their preparation, Yasuda has been assisted by specialists from the workshop of the late Henry Moore.

Kan Yasuda and Renzo Piano jointly agreed on the placement of 'Touchstones' in the piazza of Aurora Place and Yasuda hopes visitors will enjoy the white marble 'stones' visually and sensually. The 'Touchstones' he says, are made to touch.

Note: Australian Art details

Bill Henson: *Untitled 1985/86* series (includes 30 photographic images)

John Firth-Smith: *Two Fathoms 2000* (oil on linen, 8' x16')

Dale Frank: *Joaquin Phoenix (Red)* 1999 *Ryan Phillipe (Yellow)* 1999 (acrylic and varnish on linen, 136 x 116cm)

[1] Interview with Tina Tang, Project Director, Lend Lease Development.

Acknowledgements

DEVELOPER

Lend Lease Development
East Asia Property Group
Mirvac Group (Residential Only)

PROJECT MANAGER

Bovis Lend Lease

ARCHITECTS

Architect	Renzo Piano Building Workshop
	in association with
	Lend Lease Design Group (TSG)
Documentation and Interiors	Group GSA
Residential Interiors	HPA Architects
Commercial Interiors	EGO Design
	HBO EMTB Australia
	Woods Bagot
Retail Interiors	Conybeare Morrison & Partners

DESIGN CONSULTANTS

Acoustics	RFA Acoustic Design Pty Ltd
Audio Visual	Spaceage Communications
Authorities – Building Regulations	Trevor R. Howse & Associates
Civil Engineer	Jeff Moulsdale & Associates
Electrical – External lighting concept	Lighting Design Partnership
Electrical – Concept	Bovis Lend Lease (TSG)
Electrical – Residential	Flannigan Lawson Engineers
Façade	Arup Façade Engineering
Fire – Concept	Bovis Lend Lease (TSG)
Hydraulics – Concept	Bovis Lend Lease (TSG)
Hydraulics – Residential	DP Consulting Group
Hydraulic & Fire Services	The LHO Group Hydraulic & Fire Protection
Landscaping	Belt Collins Australia
Lifts	Ron Lane & Associates
Mechanical – Concept	Ove Arup
Mechanical & Electrical Services	Addicoat Hogarth Wilson
Mechanical	Jim Hatz
Structural – Tower	Lend Lease Design Group
– Steelwork and canopy	Ove Arup and Partners
Structural – Residential	Taylor, Thompson & Whitting
Signage	Minale, Tattersfield, Bryce & Partners
Specialist Lighting (Exterior Lighting)	Lighting Design Partnership

Traffic	Masson Wilson Twiney
Wind	Mel Consultants

DESIGN & CONSTRUCT SUBCONTRACTORS

Electrical – Commercial	John Goss Projects
Electrical – Residential	City Electrical
Fire Systems	Premier Fire Services
Mechanical	Environ
Hydraulics	JR Keith
Building Maintenance Unit	EW Cox
Lifts	Kone
Façade	Permasteelisa
BMCS/Security	Siemens

CONSULTANTS (GENERAL)

Planning	BBC Consulting Planners
	Conybeare Morrison & Partners
Quantity Surveyor	Rider Hunt
	Page Kirkland Partnership
	W T Partnership
Solicitors	Freehill Hollingdale & Page
	Coudert Brothers
Leasing	Finch Freeman
	Jones Lang LaSalle
Surveying	Denny Linker
	Dencon Surveying
	Higgins Norton Partners
Media	Cosway Australia Limited
	Kirby & Nolan
	Garner Maclennan Interactive
Art	Art Gallery of NSW
General Insurances	AON
Operation & Maintenance Manuals	Techscript
Testing & Certifications	Unisearch

AUTHORITIES

	City Council of Sydney
	Central Sydney Planning Committee
	Department of Urban Afairs & Planning
	Department of Public Works
	Royal Botanic Gardens
	Heritage Review Committee
	Ministry for the Arts

148 **Index**

A

2000 Olympics 38
A View from the Campidoglio, Venturi, R and
 Scott-Brown, D 127
ABC-TV 68
Abel du Petit-Thouar 29
ABN Amro 64
Academie Andre L'hote 138
Academie Moderne 138
ADM door system 88
Albini, Franco 135
Alpine Architecture, Taut, Bruno 101
Anatxu 68
Architectural Analysis 38, 56, 68
Art Gallery Road 28
Astor Flats 16, 18
Australian Subscription Library, The 22, 24

B

Banca Popolare di Lodi 44, 110, 111, 114
*Basic Writings—The Question Concerning
 Technology*, Heidegger, M 87
Belluschi, Pietro 48
Benjamin, Walter 94, 100, 101
Bennelong Point 20, 28
Bent Street 18, 20, 22, 28, 40, 42, 42, 48,
BMA House 112
BMU (Building Maintenance Unit) 130
Bonthorne, Ross 35
Boswell, James 20
Bovis Lend Lease 28, 111
Brancusi 100
Bridge Street 22
Brunelleschi 80, 87
Buchanan, P 35, 111
Buck-Morss, Susan 101
Builders and Pioneers of Australia 29
Building Maintenance Unit 130
Bureaux Publics 22
Burgin, V 101

C

Cagliari 110
Carrara 143

Centre Georges Pompidou, The 30, 122, 135
Chareau, Pierre 135
Chief Secretary's Department, The 22
Chifley Place 34
Chifley Tower 29, 38
Christian Science Monitor 29
Churchill, Bonnie 29
Circular Quay 16, 20
Cité International de Lyons 44, 110 ,111
City of Sydney, Hill, M.S 24
Cohen, Stuart 126, 127
Columbus International Exposition 110,
*Conscience of the Eye, The; The design
 and Social Life of Cities*, Sennett, R 101
Conservatorium of Music 24, 28
Contextual Piano, Tombesi, P 68
Craft of Design, The, Lampugnani, VM 111
Credito Bank 110
Crystal Palace 22

D

Debis tower 56
Denton Corker Marshall 16, 29, 38
Digital Document, The, Dyshart, B 35
Domain Parklands 24
Domain, The 28, 29
Domus 35
Dyshart, B 35

E

East Asia Property Group 18, 68
Emery Roth and Sons 48
End of Modernity, The, Vattimo, G 111, 135

F

Farm Cove 20, 22, 24
Farnsworth House, Van der Rohe, M 101
Farrer Place 34
Firth-Smith, John 136
Fonseca, Caio 136, 142
Fort Macquarie 20
Foster, Norman 135
Frampton, Kenneth 32, 35, 80, 102, 111, 111,
 122, 127

149

Frank, Dale 136, 138
Frankfurt School of Social Research 94

G

Gadamer, Hans 134, 135
Galileo 87
Garden Palace 22
Gehry, Frank 134
Genoa Columbus International Exposition
 project 44
George Street 22
Glass Architecture, Scheerbart, P 94, 101
Government Architect 1
Government House 20, 22, 29
Government Printer 24
Governor Macquarie Tower 29
Governor Phillip Tower 29, 38
Governor's Domain 20, 22
Governor-in Chief of New South Wales 20
Grace Building, The 112
GRC 110, 111
Greenway 22
Gregotti, G 135
Gregotti, Vittorio 134
Gropius, Walter 48
Ground Plane 62
Gutenberg 80

H

Habermas, Jurgen 82
Harbour Bridge, Sydney 16
Harbour Tunnel 16
Hartoonian, Gevork 80, 82, 86, 87, 135, 135
Heidegger, Martin 82, 86, 87, 102
Henson, Bill 136, 138, 143
Hill, M.S. 24
History House 22
Homo faber 80, 87
Hyde Park 20, 22

I

IBM Travelling Pavilion 32
*In Different Spaces; Place and Memory
 in Visual Culture*, Burgin, V 101

Intercontinental Hotel 22, 112
IRCAM 44, 110, 111

J

Joaquin Phoenix (Red), Frank, Dale 143
Jose, A.W 29

K

Kangaroo, Lawrence, D.H. 29
Kohn Pederson Fox 29, 38

L

La Venus 22
Lampugnani, VM 87, 111, 135
Lawrence, D.H. 24, 29
Le Corbusier 18
Lehrer, Jim 29, 101, 127
Lend lease 18, 22, 36, 136
Lend Lease Corporation 68
Lend Lease Design Group 18, 28, 34
Lend Lease Development 143
Levin, D.M, Ed 101
Lewis, Mortimer 22
Loftus Street 22
Logbook, Renzo Piano 68, 87, 94, 100, 102,
 111, 127, 135
Logistical Web 36

M

Machinatore 80, 86, 87
Macquarie Apartments 22
Macquarie Place 34
Macquarie Street 16, 18, 20, 24, 28, 22, 42,
 48, 56, 70, 74, 101, 111, 112, 114, 127
Macquarie, Lachlan, Governor 20, 22
Maison de Verrre 35
Marais quarter, The 122
Menil Museum, Houston 32, 100, 102, 110,
 111
Michelangelo 143
Miller, D 87
Miro 142
Mitchell Library 24
Modernism 94

Index

Modernity and the Hegemony of Vision, Levin, D.M, Ed 101
Mondrian 142
Moore, Henry 143
Mrs Macquarie's Chair 20
Museum of Contemporary Art, Sydney 138
Museum of Sydney 29

N

National Gallery of Victoria 138
New South Wales State Government 18
News Hour, The, with Jim Lehrrer 101, 127
Nobel, David F 87
NSW Government Printer's building 24
NSW Premier 24

O

Ontology of Construction, Hartoonian, G 80, 87, 135
Opera House, Sydney 16, 18, 20, 28, 48, 56, 68, 96, 126, 128, 134, 135, 143
Ove Arup and Partners 126

P

Pan Am Building 48,
Panoramic Views 29
Peter Buchanan 68
Phillip Lane 42, 114, 118, 127
Phillip Street 22, 29, 42, 42, 40, 106, 127
Physical Context/Cultural Context:Including it All, Cohen, S 127
'Piece by Piece', ABC TV Programme 68, 101
Pietrasanta 142, 143
Pirelli Building 48
Ponti, Gio 48
Potsdamer Platz 44, 110, 111
Potts Point 28
Prentice and Chan 142
Prentice, Tim 136, 142
Pritzker Prize 28, 87, 100
Process Architecture 35
Project Web 34, 36
Public Works Department of New South Wales 24

Q

Question Concerning Technology, The
Heidegger, Martin 82, 86

R

Religion of Technology, The: the Divinity of man and the Spirit of Invention, Nobel, David, F 87,
Renaissance 90
Renzo Piano Building Workshop (RPBW) 18, 29, 30, 32, 34 , 35, 36, 38, 44, 56, 68, 86, 90, 94, 98, 101, 110, 111, 111, 127, 132, 134, 135
Reserve Bank 18
Rice, Peter 30, 126
Rickey, George 136, 138
Rogers, Richard 30, 122, 135
Rohe, Mies, van der 101
Royal Australian College of Physicians, The 22
Royal Botanical Gardens 22, 24, 28, 58, 70, 76
Rue de Meaux 111
Rue de Meaux Housing 44, 110
Ruskin, J 82, 87

S

Sahlins, Marshall 82
Scarpa, Carlo 135
Scheerbart, Paul 94, 100, 101
Schlumberger facilities 114
Scott, Walter, Sir 20
Scott-Brown, Denise 126, 127
Seidler, Harry 16
Sennett, Richard 101
Seven Lamps of Architecture, The, Ruskin, J 87
Sharp, D 101
St James' Square 24
State Government Office Block, The 18, 24, 29
State Library, The 18, 22, 28
State Parliament 18
Stock Exchange 16
Structural Framing 50

Sustainable Architectures 68
Sydney Biennale 138
Sydney Cove 20, 28
Sydney Harbour 64
Sydney Hospital 18
Tang, Tina 143
Taut, Bruno 101
Tectonic Culture, studies in, Frampton, K
  35, 80, 111
Thierry, de 22
Tjibaou Cultural Centre, New Caledonia 100
Tombesi, Paolo 68
Treasury, The New South Wales 22
Truth and Method, Gadamer 135
Two Fathoms, Firth-Smith, John 143

U

UME 68
Utzon, Jorn 18, 28, 48, 56, 126, 134

V

van Dieman's land 20
Vattimo, G 111, 135
Venice Biennale 138
Venturi, Robert 126, 127
Victoria Street 28
Victoria, Queen 24
Viollet-le-Duc 82
Voyage autour du monde sur la fregate
  La Venus, pendant les années 29

W

Woolloomooloo Bay 20
World War 82

Y

Yale University 142
Yasuda, Kan 114, 136, 136, 142, 143
York Street 28
Young Street 22

Z

Zabalbeascoa 68

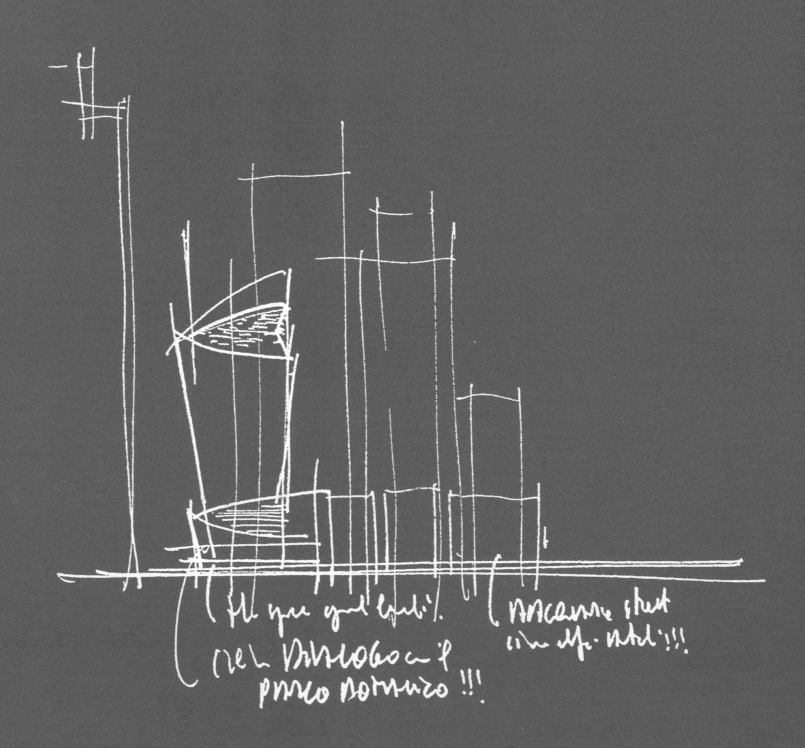